W0238426

To the Teacher

Non-native English speakers who enroll in a college or university want to develop writing skills that will lead to academic success. This book is a combination text and workbook. Its focused lessons, specific exercises, and ample opportunities for practice are designed to help your students gain confidence in writing academic prose.

This new edition of *Writing Essays* is designed to take university-level students with an intermediate ability in English as a second language from paragraph writing through essay writing. The course combines a process approach to writing (where students work on invention, peer response, editing, and writing multiple drafts) with a pragmatic approach to teaching the basics of writing (with direct instruction on such elements as topic sentences, thesis statements, and outlines).

The Introduction presents process writing to students. The tasks in the main units are graded. Students first work on recognizing and identifying key writing structures from model paragraphs and essays. Then they manipulate the structures in short, manageable tasks. Finally, they apply the structures to their own writing. There are opportunities for students to work independently, with a partner, and with a group. The exercises can be done either in class or as homework. Critical thinking is emphasized, so that students become aware of the impact of their choice of words, sentences, and organizational techniques on the effectiveness of their writing. The focus throughout is on academic writing—the type of writing used in university courses and exams in English-speaking institutions of higher learning.

In Units 1–6, students analyze and write the types of paragraphs that commonly occur in academic contexts. They practice writing topic sentences and concluding sentences, organizing the paragraph coherently, and using appropriate vocabulary, grammar, and transitional devices in the paragraph body. In Unit 7, students write two-paragraph papers, in preparation for longer assignments. In Units 8–11, students apply what they have learned about paragraphs to essay writing. They work on developing and supporting a central thesis, organizing an outline from which to write, and writing effective introductions and conclusions. Unit 12 discusses strategies for timed essay writing, including understanding standard instructions, time-management techniques, and methods for organizing information.

Included in the Student Book are samples of the development of an essay from brainstorming to the final draft. There is also a guide to punctuation and examples of a letter requesting information, a personal essay of the type commonly required in college applications, and a résumé.

The Teacher's Guide supports the instructor by offering teaching suggestions, a discussion of marking and grading writing, ideas for supplemental activities for each unit, and photocopiable exercises and activities.

To the Student

Writing is a very important part of your university study. You will write assignments that may range from one paragraph to several pages long, and will write answers on tests and exams that may be a few sentences long or a complete essay.

Academic writing in English may be different not only from academic writing in your own language, but even from other writing in English. The purpose of this new edition of *Writing Essays* is to help you recognize and produce the sort of writing that you will do for your university courses.

During this course, you will have many opportunities to study and discuss examples of English academic writing. Naturally, you will also have many opportunities to discuss your own academic writing and the writing of your classmates. You will learn how important the reader is to the writer, and how to express clearly and directly what you mean to communicate. We hope that what you learn in this course will help you throughout your academic studies and beyond.

You should come to your writing class every day with energy and a willingness to work and learn. Your instructor and your classmates have much to share with you, and you have much to share with them. By coming to class with your questions, taking chances and trying new ways, and expressing your ideas in another language, you will add not only to your own world but to the world of those around you.

Good luck!

Dorothy E Zemach
Lisa A Ghulldu

Introduction: Process Writing

In this unit, you will ...

- **learn about process writing, the writing method used in most English-speaking university classes.**

The writing process

1 These words are important for understanding the writing process. Match each word with the correct definition.

a. step	**1.** to check a piece of writing for errors
b. topic	**2.** a group of related sentences
c. gather	**3.** one thing in a series of things you do
d. organize	**4.** subject; what the piece of writing is about
e. paragraph	**5.** to change or correct a piece of writing
f. essay	**6.** a short piece of writing, at least three paragraphs long
g. proofread	**7.** to arrange in a clear, logical way
h. edit	**8.** to find and collect together

The six steps of the writing process

2 **Read about the writing process. These are the steps you will practice in this book.**

➲ **Process writing**

When we write, we do more than just put words together to make sentences. Good writers go through several steps to produce a piece of writing.

Pre-writing

STEP ONE: Choose a topic. Before you write, your teacher gives you a specific assignment or some ideas of what to write about. If not, choose your topic yourself.

STEP TWO: Gather ideas. When you have a topic, think about what you will write about that topic.

STEP THREE: Organize. Decide which of the ideas you want to use and where you want to use them. Choose which idea to talk about first, which to talk about next, and which to talk about last.

Drafting

STEP FOUR: Write. Write your paragraph or essay from start to finish. Use your notes about your ideas and organization.

Reviewing and revising

STEP FIVE: Review structure and content. Check what you have written. Read your writing silently to yourself or aloud, perhaps to a friend. Look for places where you can add more information, and check to see if you have any unnecessary information. Ask a classmate to exchange papers with you. Your classmate reads your paper, and you read his or hers. Getting a reader's opinion is a good way to know if your writing is clear and effective. Learning to give opinions about other people's writing helps you to improve your own. You may want to go on to step six now and revise the structure and content of your paper before you proofread it.

Rewriting

STEP SIX:

Revise structure and content. Use your ideas from step five to re-write your text, making improvements to the structure and content. You might need to explain something more clearly, or add more details. You may even need to change your organization so that your paper is more logical. Together, steps five and six can be called *editing*.

Proofread. Read your paper again. This time, check your spelling and grammar and think about the words you have chosen to use.

Make final corrections. Check that you have corrected the errors you discovered in steps five and six and make any other changes you want to make. Now your text is finished!

Steps five and six can be repeated many times.

Review

3 **Complete this chart, summarizing the steps of the writing process.**

Pre-writing

- **STEP ONE:** Choose a ....
- **STEP TWO:** Gather ....
- **STEP THREE:** Decide ....

Drafting

- **STEP FOUR:** Write ....

Reviewing and revising

- **STEP FIVE:** Check ....

Rewriting

- **STEP SIX:**

May need to ... ■ explain ....

■ add ....

■ change ....

Steps .... and .... may be .... many times.

1 Pre-Writing: Getting Ready to Write

In this unit, you will learn how to …

- **choose and narrow a topic.**
- **gather ideas.**
- **edit ideas.**

➲ What is pre-writing?

Before you begin writing, you decide what you are going to write about. Then you plan what you are going to write. This process is called *pre-writing*.

Choosing and narrowing a topic

➲ How to choose a topic for a paragraph

A paragraph is a group of five to ten sentences that give information about a topic. Before you write, you must choose a topic for your paragraph.

- Choose a topic that isn't too *narrow* (limited, brief). A narrow topic will not have enough ideas to write about. *The ages of my brothers and sisters* is too narrow. You can't write very much about it.
- Choose a topic that isn't too *broad* (general). A broad topic will have too many ideas for just one paragraph. Most paragraphs are five to ten sentences long. *Schools* is too general. There are thousands of things you could say about it.

A student could narrow this topic by choosing one aspect of schools to discuss.

schools → *high schools in my country*
popular school clubs
university entrance exams

1 Choose three topics from this list. Narrow each of the three down to a paragraph topic. Then compare with a partner.

a. holidays
b. friends
c. my country
d. dancing
e. cars

Brainstorming

➲ **What is brainstorming?**

Brainstorming is a way of gathering ideas about a topic. Think of a storm: thousands of drops of rain, all coming down together. Now, imagine thousands of ideas "raining" down onto your paper! When you brainstorm, write down every idea that comes to you. Don't worry now about whether the ideas are good or silly, useful or not. You can decide that later. Right now, you are gathering as many ideas as you can.

You will learn three types of brainstorming in this unit: *making a list*, *freewriting*, and *mapping*.

➲ **Making a list**

Write single words, phrases, or sentences that are connected to your topic. Look at this list a student made when brainstorming ideas to write about her topic, "What should I study in college?"

history—learning about the past
math (too difficult, not interesting?)
What job do I want later?
English for work? Travel?
writing?
science—biology, chemistry
I don't like physics!
journalism
I like reading—literature?
art—drawing, painting, sculpture
photography?
studying / homework
friends / social life

2 **Work with a partner or small group. Choose one of these topics. List as many ideas as you can in five minutes.**

a. teenage fashions

b. social networking

c. driving a motorcycle

3 **Work alone. Choose a topic from exercise 1 on page 5, and list as many ideas as you can in five minutes.**

Freewriting

When you freewrite, you write whatever comes into your head about your topic, without stopping. Most freewriting exercises are short—just five or ten minutes.

Freewriting helps you practice *fluency* (writing quickly and easily). When you freewrite, you do not need to worry about *accuracy* (having correct grammar and spelling). Don't check your dictionary when you freewrite. Don't stop if you make a mistake. Just keep writing!

Here is an example of a student's freewriting:

> *There are ~~too~~ so many subjects to study at university, it is difficult to choose one for my major. I've always made good grades in math, but I don't like it very much. I don't like ~~physical~~ physics or any science very much. Writing—I've always liked writing. Would journalism be a good course to take? Newspapers have pictures, too, so maybe photography would be good. I'm ~~maybe~~ definitely looking forward to meeting new friends at university. And what about reading? Reading is a part of any course, but literature includes a lot of reading and it probably includes a lot of writing, too.*

Notice how the writer's ideas jump around. When she makes a mistake, she just crosses it out and continues writing. One thought (*writing*) leads to another (*journalism*), and then to another (*photography*). There are some details that are not exactly about her topic (*looking forward to meeting new friends*), but that's OK in freewriting. You want to get as many ideas on paper as you can. You can take out unnecessary words and sentences later.

4 **Choose one of the narrowed topics you thought of for exercise 1 on page 5. Practice freewriting for five minutes. Remember, do not stop, erase, or go back. Just write as much as you can.**

Mapping

To make a map, use a whole sheet of paper, and write your topic in the middle, with a circle around it. Then put the next idea in a circle above or below your topic, and connect the circles with lines. The lines show that the two ideas are related.

The example below shows a map of "What should I study in college?" The writer connected *favorite subjects* to the main idea. *Art* and *English* are connected to *favorite subjects* to show that they are related.

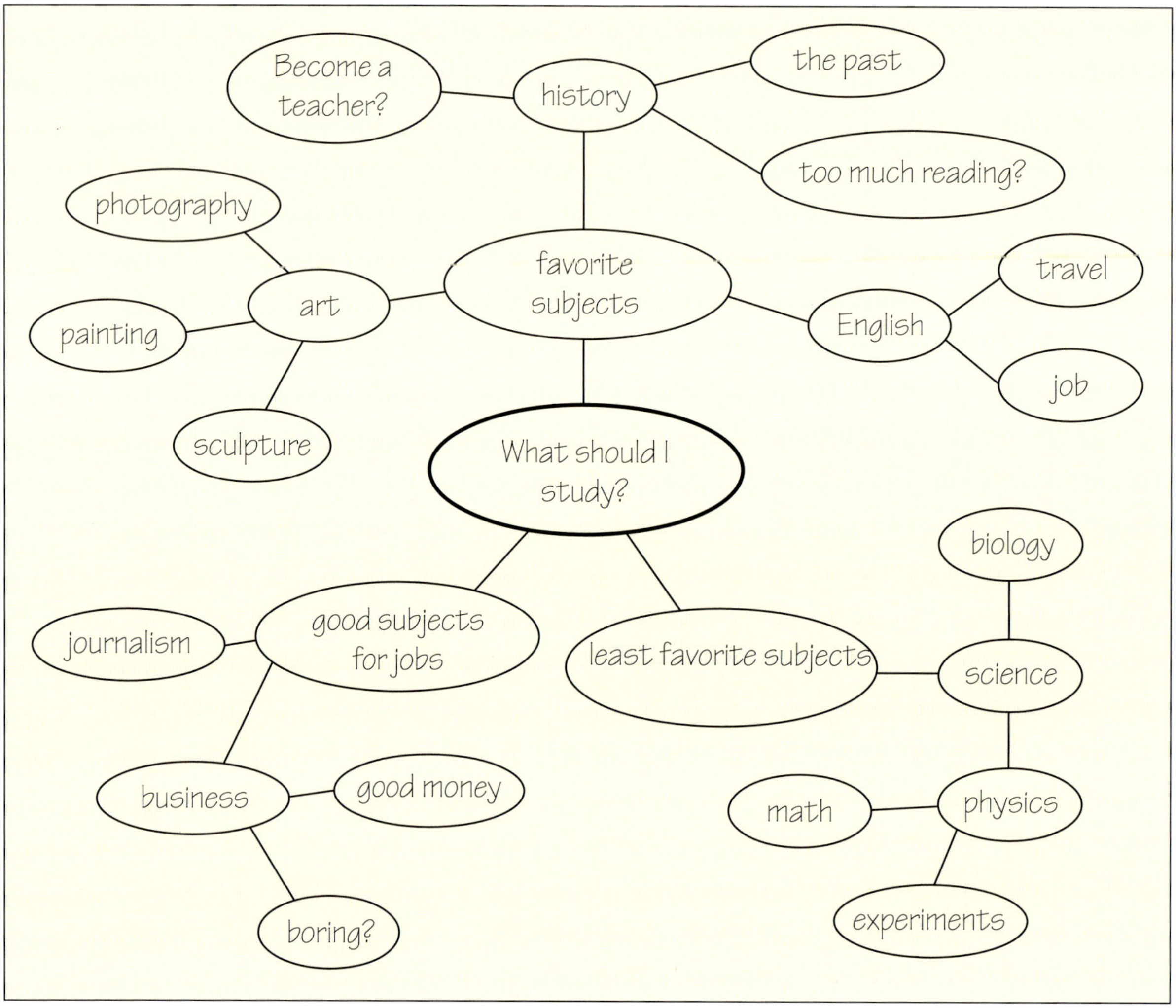

5 **Choose another narrowed topic you thought of for exercise 1 on page 5. Make a map in five minutes. Share your map with a partner. Explain how the circles are related to each other.**

What's the best way to brainstorm?

There is no best method of brainstorming. Some writers like to use lists because they don't have to write complete sentences. Some writers like freewriting because they can write quickly and ideas come easily. Some writers prefer mapping because they can easily see the relationship between ideas. Experiment with all three methods, and then choose the one that works best for you.

Editing

➲ How to edit

After you have gathered plenty of ideas, you will need to go back and edit them. This is the time to choose which ideas are the most interesting, and which are the most *relevant to* (important or necessary for) your topic. Of course, you can still add new ideas if you think of something else while you are re-reading your list. For example, the student writing "What should I study in college?" edited her list like this:

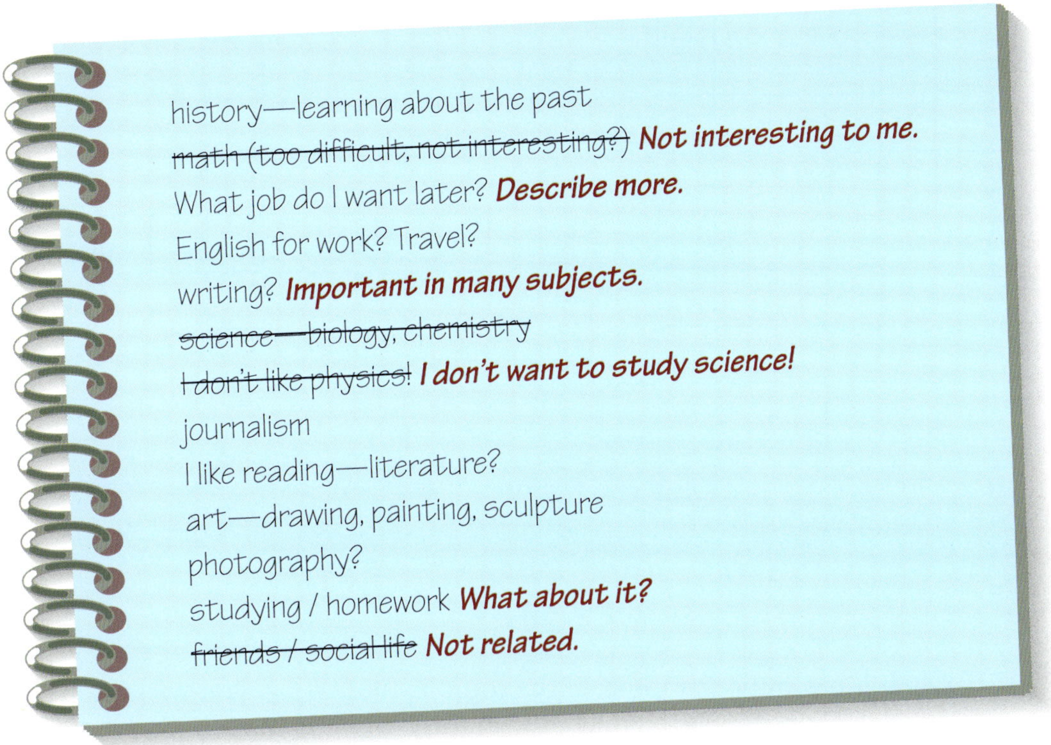

To edit freewriting, cross out sentences or parts of sentences that aren't related. You can add more ideas in the margin or add more sentences at the bottom. To edit a map, cross out circles that don't belong, and add new ones if you get more ideas. You might also change the lines you have drawn.

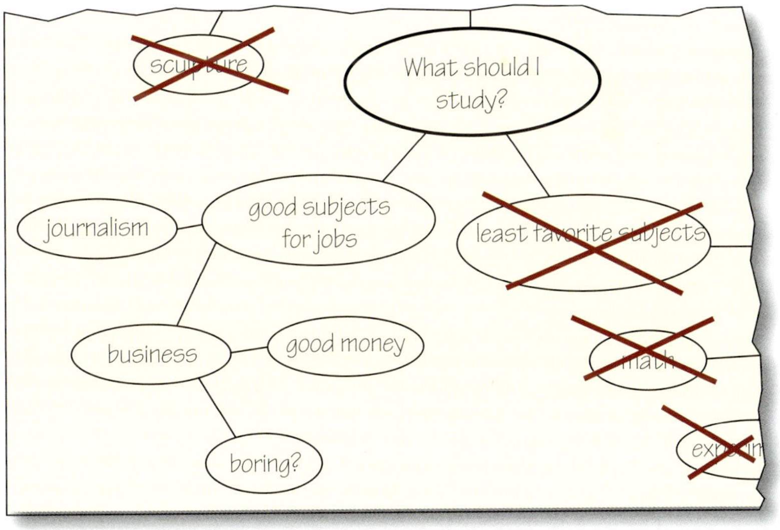

6 **Look at the list you made in exercise 3 on page 6, the freewriting you did in exercise 4 on page 7, or the map you made in exercise 5 on page 8. Edit your brainstorming. Show your work to a partner. Explain how you edited your brainstorming.**

Review

7 **Complete the crossword puzzle.**

Each paragraph has only one topic. If the topic is too [1] n___, you will not be able to write enough about it. On the other hand, if the topic is too [2] b___, you will have too many ideas for just one paragraph.

After you choose a topic, you will need to [3] b___ some ideas to write about in your paragraph. One way to do this is to make a [4] l___. Another way of brainstorming is [5] m___. After you have written down many ideas, you can go back and decide which ones are the most interesting and the most [6] r___ to your topic.

[7] F___ is a useful way to help you write more easily and naturally. In this kind of writing, you are working on [8] f___, and not [9] a___.

8 **Look again at the note about brainstorming at the bottom of page 8. Brainstorm a list of pros (good things) and cons (bad things) about each of the three methods of brainstorming.**

2 The Structure of a Paragraph

In this unit, you will learn ...

- **the definition of a paragraph.**
- **the parts of a paragraph.**
- **how to identify and write topic sentences.**

➲ What is a paragraph?

As you learned in Unit 1, a paragraph is a group of sentences about a single *topic*. Together, the sentences of the paragraph explain the writer's *main idea* (most important idea) about the topic. In academic writing, a paragraph is often between five and ten sentences long, but it can be longer or shorter, depending on the topic. The first sentence of a paragraph is usually indented (moved in) a few spaces.

Understanding a paragraph

1 **Read this paragraph. It is the beginning of an article about Switzerland in a student newspaper. Then answer the questions.**

Switzerland—Something Interesting at Every Turn

By Ken Jones

If you dream of traveling to a country with beautiful mountains, delicious food, wonderful places to go sight-seeing, and polite people, you should visit Switzerland. If you look at the map, the first thing you notice is that Switzerland has many mountains, including some of the highest in Europe. Climbing or skiing down the mountains is great fun. Another thing you will notice is that Switzerland shares its borders with five different countries: France, Germany, Italy, Austria, and Lichtenstein. In fact, there are four official languages in Switzerland: German, French, Italian, and Romansch. All these groups of people make Swiss culture very interesting. Finally, Switzerland has many cities and interesting places to visit. Cities such as Bern have modern buildings like the Paul Klee Zentrum, yet the traditional alpine refuges in the mountains show that the country's old traditions are still alive. All the people, places, and things to see make Switzerland a great place for a holiday.

a. What is the topic of the paragraph?

....

b. What is the main idea about the topic?

....

c. What ideas help explain the main idea?

....

....

....

Paragraph organization

➲ What makes a paragraph?

A paragraph has three basic parts:

1. The topic sentence. This is the main idea of the paragraph. It is usually the first sentence of the paragraph, and it is the most general sentence of the paragraph.

2. The supporting sentences. These are sentences that talk about or explain the topic sentence. They are more detailed ideas that follow the topic sentence.

3. The concluding sentence. This may be found as the last sentence of a paragraph. It can finish a paragraph by repeating the main idea or just giving a final comment about the topic.2

2 **Read the paragraph about Switzerland in exercise 1 on page 11 again. Circle the topic sentence, put one line under the supporting sentences, and put two lines under the concluding sentence.**

3 **Put a check (✓) next to the group of sentences that makes a good paragraph. Why are the other groups of sentences not good paragraphs?**

a. ☐

Many people suffer from insomnia, which is the inability to fall asleep or stay asleep. There are several causes of insomnia. One of the main causes is stress. When people feel stressed or nervous about their work, for example, they may not be able to fall asleep for many hours or they may wake up during the night and not be able to fall asleep again. When people do not have enough sleep, it can affect their mood, making them irritable or depressed. Insomnia can also have a negative effect on concentration and job performance. Therefore, finding help for insomnia is very important for people who suffer from it.

b. ☐

Classes in literature are useful no matter what job you intend to have when you finish university. Books are about life. People who study literature learn the skill of reading carefully and understanding characters, situations, and relationships. This kind of understanding can be useful to teachers and business people alike. Literature classes also require a lot of writing, so they help students develop the skill of clear communication. Of course, a professional writer needs to have this skill, but it is an equally important skill for an engineer. Finally, reading literature helps develop an understanding of many different points of view. Reading a novel by a Russian author, for example, will help a reader learn more about Russian culture. For anyone whose job may bring them into contact with Russian colleagues, this insight can help encourage better cross-cultural understanding. Studying literature is studying life, so it is relevant to almost any job you can think of.

c. ☐

One good way to learn another language is to live in a country where that language is used. When you live in another country, the language is around you all the time, so you can learn to listen to and speak it more easily.

The topic and the main idea

➲ The topic sentence …

- usually comes first in a paragraph.
- gives the writer's main idea or opinion about the topic and helps the reader understand what the paragraph is going to talk about.

4 Circle the topic of the sentence. Underline the main idea about the topic.

a. (Switzerland) is a <u>very interesting country to visit</u>.

b. One cause of insomnia is stress.

c. A library is a good place to study.

d. Learning a second language creates job opportunities.

e. Watching and playing sports can both be good forms of relaxation.

f. One of the most valuable tools for students is the computer.

g. People with different personalities may find it difficult to live together.

h. The summer season is a good time for travel.

i. There are several advantages to living in a larger city.

5 For each of these paragraphs, choose the sentence from the list below that would make the best topic sentence.

a.

....

.... When Ken wanted to enter a good university, he studied hard to pass the examination. The first time he took the exam, he did not do well, and he felt very discouraged. But he knew he wanted to study at that university, so he studied more. The next year, he tried taking the exam again. The second time, he did very well, and now he is studying engineering. I believe Ken is a good role model for me, and he has taught me that never giving up is the best way to succeed.

1. One of my closest friends, named Ken, is a person I can trust.
2. My friend Ken is a very successful student.
3. I admire my friend Ken because he doesn't give up.

b.

.... *Many children begin learning to play soccer when they are very young. You often can see them playing at school or in the streets around their houses. In high school, students may play soccer on a team and compete in tournaments. If a player is very good, he might go on to play for a professional team. People in my country love to watch soccer on television and also go to the games whenever they can. Many people have a favorite team or player, and everyone loves to talk about matches and competitions. Soccer is really like a national sport in my country.*

1. I love to play soccer, and I hope I can become a professional player one day.
2. There are many popular sports in my country, but the most popular sport is soccer.
3. Soccer is a difficult sport to learn to play well.

6 **Write a topic sentence for three of these topics.**

a. A benefit of doing physical exercise
b. A popular holiday or celebration
c. A healthy food to eat
d. A benefit of learning a second language
e. Playing a musical instrument

topic: ....

....

....

topic: ....

....

....

topic: ....

....

....

Review

7 **These sentences are mixed up parts of one paragraph. Number the parts in order: 1. topic sentence, 2. supporting sentences, and 3. concluding sentence.**

What should I study at university?

a. .... *It wasn't an easy decision, but for the reasons listed above, I have decided to study journalism.*

b. .... *It can be difficult to choose a subject to study in college because there are so many choices, but by considering my skills and interests, I have decided to study journalism.*

c. .... *I have always enjoyed writing, so it is sensible to choose a major that involves writing. When I begin working, I would like to have the opportunity to travel, and travel is often an important part of a journalist's job. Finally, I am also interested in photography, and pictures are very important in journalism.*

8 **Use words or phrases in the box to complete the sentences.**

concluding sentence	indented	main idea	paragraph
supporting sentences	topic	topic sentence	

a. The .... is usually the first sentence in a .... It gives the .... and the ....

b. The first sentence of a paragraph should be ....

c. The .... come after the topic sentence, and they explain the topic sentence.

d. The .... comes at the end of a paragraph.

3 The Development of a Paragraph

In this unit, you will learn ...

- **methods of paragraph support and development.**
- **how to write concluding sentences.**
- **how to do peer editing.**

Paragraph development

After you have chosen a topic and written a topic sentence, you *develop* your main idea by adding more information to explain what you mean. This unit will explain three common ways to develop a paragraph: giving *details*, giving an *explanation*, and giving an *example*.

Details

1 Details are specific points that tell more about a general statement. Read this brochure from a health club. Notice the details that help develop the paragraph.

ATLAS HEALTH CENTER

You'll love working out at the Atlas Health Center, and you'll love what it does for you! We have state-of-the-art exercise equipment in large, air-conditioned rooms. You can work out alone or with the help of one of our professional personal trainers. If you like to exercise with friends, join an aerobics or swimming class—or even try kickboxing! Our staff nutrition experts are always on hand to talk with you about health issues. When you've finished, you can relax with a whirlpool bath or a sauna. Come exercise with us at Atlas, and you'll soon be feeling strong and looking good.

2 In the paragraph above, underline the topic sentence. Below, list the details used to support the topic sentence. Compare your answers with a partner.

a. ....

b. ....

c. ....

d. ....

e. ....

f. ....

Explanation

3 **An explanation tells what something means or how something works. In this paragraph, underline the topic sentence. Then answer the questions.**

"A stitch in time saves nine." My mother, who likes to sew, used this simple saying to teach me the value of working on problems when they are still small. Originally, the saying referred to sewing—if you have a small hole in a shirt, you can repair it with one stitch. But if you wait, the hole will get larger, and it will take you nine stitches. This simple sentence reminds me to take care of small problems before they become big problems.

a. What is the writer trying to explain? ....

b. Is she successful? Do you understand the explanation? yes / no

Example

4 **An example is a specific person, place, thing, or event that supports an idea or statement. This paragraph includes an example from the writer's own experience. Underline the topic sentence.**

Even when two people get off on the wrong foot, they can become good friends. When I was a university student, I lived in the dormitory for the first year, with a roommate. I arrived a few days before he did. When he first came, he woke me up at 3:00 in the morning making a lot of noise. He was cooking dinner! When I got up in the morning to make myself breakfast, I found his dirty dishes left on the counters and in the sink. I was very annoyed. However, when I met him later that afternoon, he was very nice. He apologized for leaving a mess, and explained that he had had some trouble with his airplane flights and had been traveling for a long time. He was hungry when he arrived and very sleepy. After that, he was always good about washing his dishes. He was in two of my classes, and we often studied together. We're not roommates anymore, but we are still friends.

5 **Why do you think the writer chose to use an example to develop the paragraph in exercise 4 above? Write your reason here, and then compare with a partner.**

....

Choosing a means of support

6 **Would you develop each of these topics with details, an explanation, or an example? Explain your choices to a partner. (More than one answer is possible.)**

a. what freedom means to me

b. an unusual vacation

c. weddings in my country

d. why I don't like to swim

e. the ideal job

7 **Develop your own paragraph. Look back at the topic sentences you wrote in Unit 2, exercise 6 on page 15. Follow these steps.**

Step one: Choose one that you would like to develop into a paragraph.

Step two: Brainstorm some ideas using any method you like.

Step three: Develop your paragraph with supporting sentences.

Step four: Exchange paragraphs with a partner. Say what kind of support your partner used. Could your partner tell what kind of support you used?

Concluding sentences

How to end a paragraph

The final sentence of a paragraph is called the *concluding sentence*. It sums up the main points or restates the main idea in a different way. A sentence that sums up the paragraph reminds the reader of what the writer's main idea and supporting points were. A sentence that restates the main idea should give the same information in a slightly different way, perhaps by using different words or by using different word order. A concluding sentence should not introduce a new point.

8 **Read the example paragraphs in exercises 3 and 4 on page 18 again. Underline the concluding sentences. Do the concluding sentences sum up the information in the paragraph or restate the main idea?**

9 **Work with a partner. Take turns reading these paragraphs aloud. Is the main idea developed by details, an explanation, or an example? Is there a concluding sentence? Circle *yes* or *no*. If there is no concluding sentence, write one with your partner.**

Even simple study habits can improve your grades. In college, I learned how important it is to get enough sleep. When you are well-rested, it is easier to learn. Research shows that when people don't get enough sleep, their memories aren't as effective. If students are really tired, they might even fall asleep in class! It's easy to see how getting enough sleep can improve your performance in school.

a. means of support: ....

concluding sentence? yes / no

....

My favorite class is psychology. I enjoy learning about the ways people think and behave. I also am interested in learning about the way children's minds develop.

b. means of support: ....
concluding sentence? yes / no
....

I am too nervous to sing karaoke songs with my friends. The last time I tried was on my birthday, when my friends took me to a karaoke club. I told my friends I didn't want to sing, but they encouraged me until I said yes. When I stood up in front of the microphone, I was so scared, I felt dizzy. It was hard to hear the music, and my mouth was too dry to make a sound. I just stood there until a friend jumped up next to me and finished the song.

c. means of support: ....
concluding sentence? yes / no
....

I will never eat dinner at The Little French Bistro again. The restaurant is not very clean. You can see dust in the corners and on the shelves. The food is expensive, but the portions are small. I never feel full after I've finished eating. In addition, the waiters are not very friendly. For these reasons, I will not visit that restaurant again.

d. means of support: ....
concluding sentence? yes / no
....

For me, a friend is someone who accepts you the way you are. A friend doesn't want you to change your personality or your style. I like people who don't care if the people they are with are wearing popular clothes or listening to trendy music.

e. means of support: ....
concluding sentence? yes / no
....

Peer editing

➲ What is peer editing?

Showing your work to another student is a very useful way to improve your writing. This is called *peer editing*. You read your partner's writing and your partner reads yours. You comment on your partner's writing and your partner comments on yours. You might talk together, write comments on a sheet that your instructor gives you, or write directly on your partner's paper.

Here is the first draft of the paragraph about the writer and his friend. The writer has shown the paragraph to another student, who wrote some comments.

Topic sentence
I don't know the meaning of this idiom.
Even when two people get off on the wrong foot, they can still
Developed by example
become good friends. When I was a university student, I lived in the
What was his name?
dormitory for the first year, with a roommate. I arrived a few days before
Did you meet him then?
he did. When he first came, he woke me up at 3:00 in the morning making
How did you know he was cooking?
a lot of noise. He was cooking dinner! When I got up in the morning to
How did you feel about that?
make myself breakfast, I found his dirty dishes left on the counters and in
Explain how you noticed this
the sink. However, later, he was very nice. He apologized for leaving a
but why did he arrive so late?
mess, and explained that he was hungry when he arrived and very sleepy.
After that, he was always good about washing his dishes. He was in two
good example
of my classes, and we often studied together. We're not roommates
anymore, but we are still friends.

10 Look at the handwritten comments on the paragraph above, and answer these questions with a partner.

a. Why do you think the peer editor sometimes wrote questions instead of statements? For example, why did she write "What was his name?" instead of "Tell me his name"?

b. Why do you think the peer editor marked the topic sentence and the concluding sentence?

c. The peer editor didn't understand a phrase in the topic sentence. Do you think the writer should change that sentence? Why or why not?

d. Go back to exercise 4 on page 18 and read the paragraph again. Did the writer use the reader's suggestions?

➲ Why do writers use peer editing?

There are two reasons for peer editing. The first is to get a reader's opinion about your writing. A reader can tell you that …

- you should add more details or explanation.
- something is not organized clearly.
- you have some information that is not relevant.
- there is something that is hard to understand.

These comments will help you write your next draft. Remember that suggestions from a peer editor are just suggestions. You don't have to make every change that is suggested. However, you should think about all of the comments that you receive.

The second reason to share writing with others is for you to read more examples of writing. Other people will have had experiences that you haven't. They may show you fresh ways of writing about experiences. Reading their paragraphs and essays can give you good ideas to use yourself in the future.

➲ How do I peer edit?

- Read your partner's paper several times. The first time, just read from the beginning through to the end. Ask yourself, "What is it about? What is the writer's purpose?"
- On your second reading, go more slowly and look at specific parts of the writing and make notes.
  - Look for topic sentences and concluding sentences.
  - Note places where you have trouble understanding something, where there seems to be unnecessary information, or where there is not enough information.
  - Let the writer know which parts of the paper are especially strong or interesting.
  - Ask questions. This is a good way to let the writer know where he or she could add more information.
  - Circle or underline words, phrases, and sentences that you wish to comment on.
- Don't look for grammar or spelling mistakes. Pay attention just to the content and organization of the paper.

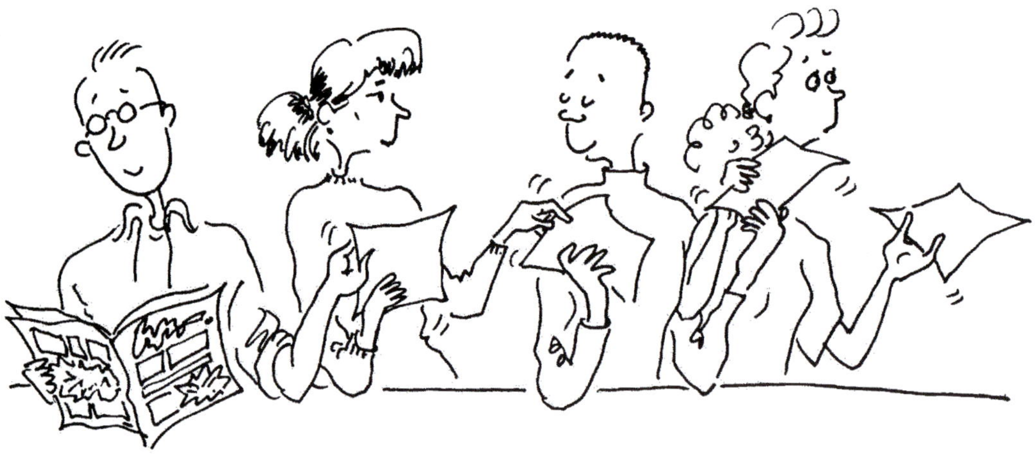

Giving constructive suggestions

11 For each pair of sentences, check (✓) the one that you feel would be most helpful to the writer. Share your answers with a partner, and explain your choices.

a. ☐ This is a weak topic sentence.
☐ Can you make this topic sentence stronger?

b. ☐ Did you remember a concluding sentence?
☐ Why didn't you write a concluding sentence?

c. ☐ You didn't write enough.
☐ Please explain more about your vacation. Where did you stay? What did you do during the day?

d. ☐ I'm not sure what this part means.
☐ This must be wrong. I can't understand it.

e. ☐ I think this sentence should come before the next one.
☐ Your organization is pretty bad. You'd better change it.

f. ☐ Why do you keep saying the same thing over and over again?
☐ I think these two sentences are really saying the same thing.

g. ☐ I can't understand why you're talking about your sister.
☐ Your paragraph is about your brother, but this sentence is about your sister. Are you sure it's relevant?

h. ☐ This is a good paragraph. Nice job! I wish I could write as well as you.
☐ I like your topic sentence because it has a strong main idea. Your example is funny. I wish I could meet your brother!

12 Read this paragraph aloud with a partner. Then peer edit it together. Then join another pair and share your comments.

My father is a teacher. I admire him a lot. I am considering becoming a teacher, too. My older brother works for a big company. My father really loves learning, so he is a natural teacher. My father always helped me with my homework. I guess I will become a teacher.

13 **Write a second draft of the paragraph in exercise 12 on page 23. Use the comments you and your partner made. Then exchange paragraphs with your partner. Discuss how your versions are different from the original. Do you think the second drafts are better? Why or why not?**

Review

14 **Read these statements. Write T (true) or F (false). If the statement is false, change it to make it true. Then compare your answers with a partner.**

a. .... Details give more specific information than the topic sentence.

b. .... An explanation tells what something is or how it works.

c. .... A detail is usually a short, personal story.

d. .... The concluding sentence uses the same words as the topic sentence.

e. .... The concluding sentence should finish the paragraph with a new idea.

f. .... A peer editor should mark any spelling and grammatical mistakes carefully.

g. .... A peer editor should give some positive comments.

h. .... Peer editing helps the writer, not the reader.

i. .... If a peer editor can't understand something that you wrote, then you know he or she isn't a very good reader.

j. .... A peer editor should be able to identify your topic sentence, main idea, and concluding sentence easily.

4 Descriptive Paragraphs

In this unit, you will learn about ...

- **descriptive paragraphs and reasons for writing them.**
- **organizing and writing descriptive paragraphs using adjectives and prepositions.**
- **using connecting words and phrases to write a paragraph that describes a process.**

➲ Describing people, places, and processes

A descriptive paragraph explains how someone or something looks or feels. A process paragraph explains how something is done.

Describing a place

➲ Using adjectives

Adjectives are words that tell us how things look, feel, taste, sound, or smell. Adjectives also describe how you feel about something. Here are a few common adjectives.

shape and size	atmosphere	how you feel	appearance
large / small	cozy	amazed	colorful
wide / narrow	comfortable	surprised	unforgettable
round	warm / cool	happy	beautiful
rectangular	cold / hot	nostalgic	unattractive

A description of a place may answer some of these questions:

- Where is the place?
- How big is it?
- How warm or cold is the place?
- How does the place make you feel? Why?
- What things can you see in this place?
- What colors do you see?

1 List some words to describe these places.

2 **Read this description from a travel brochure. Circle the adjectives.**

Niagara Falls, a popular destination for thousands of visitors each year, is a beautiful place. When you stand at the edge and look down at the 188 feet of white waterfalls, you feel amazed at the power of nature. The tree-lined river that leads into the falls is fast-moving, pouring over the edge of the falls and crashing to the bottom in a loud roar. If you want to experience the falls close up, go for a boat ride. You'll come near enough to look up at the roaring streams of water flowing over the edge and feel the cool mist that rises as the water hits the rocks below. Seeing Niagara Falls is an unforgettable experience!

Using prepositions

Prepositions tell us how a space is organized. These are some common and useful prepositions and phrasal prepositions:

in front of / in back of, behind
on top of / on the bottom of
next to
above / below, underneath

to the right of / to the left of
in the middle of
around
between

3 **Read this paragraph that describes someone's favorite place. Underline the prepositions.**

My favorite place to relax is a small café down the street from where I live. This café is on a small side street and as soon as you see it, you feel like going in. There are three windows on either side of the door, and each window has a small window box with brightly colored flowers. There is a small wooden door that opens into the café, and as you go in, you can see a dozen small tables all around the room. Even though it isn't a big place, its size makes it very cozy and comfortable. I always like to sit at a small table in the corner near the front windows. From here, I can look at the artwork on the walls and at the pretty green plants hanging from the ceiling. With a strong cup of coffee and a good book, I feel very happy and relaxed in my favorite café.

4 **Write six sentences to describe the place where you are right now. Try to answer some of the questions under "Using adjectives" on page 25. Use adjectives and prepositions.**

Describing a character

➲ Describing people

Here are some common adjectives for describing people:

Personality	*Physical characteristics*
happy, satisfied	big, large, tall
relaxed	small, tiny, short
exciting	thin
nervous	heavy
angry	strong
serious	weak
sad, depressed	brown-, black-, blond-, red-haired
outgoing	light-, dark-skinned
....	....
....	....

A description of a person may answer some of the following questions:

- Who is the person?
- What does the person do?
- What does he or she look like?
- How does the person act—how is his or her personality?
- How does he or she make others feel?

5 **With a partner, add at least two other adjectives to the two lists above.**

6 **Read this description written by a young woman about her grandmother. Circle the adjectives that describe the grandmother.**

When I was young, I admired my grandmother for her strength and kindness. She was not very big. In fact, she was tiny and very thin. She was strong, though. She lived by herself and still did a lot of the chores around her house. When I was a child, I saw her almost every day, and she and I would talk about everything. She was a very happy person and was always smiling and joking, and she often made me laugh. My grandmother was also very patient, and she would listen to all of my problems. She gave me very good advice whenever I needed it. I didn't need to be afraid to tell her anything, because she never got mad at me. She just listened and tried to help. I also liked to spend time with her because she had interesting stories to tell about her own childhood and life experiences. When I was young, my grandmother was my favorite friend.

7 **Describe one of these people. Write eight sentences. Try to answer three or more of the questions at the bottom of page 27. Use your imagination!**

8 **Think of a person or place you know well. Then brainstorm your ideas, narrow your topic, and write a descriptive paragraph.**

Describing a process

9 **A process paragraph is a description of how something works or how something is done. It explains the steps you need to follow to complete an activity. Read the following science experiment and do the exercises below.**

Evaporation is the process of changing from a liquid to a vapor. A simple experiment can be done to learn more about how evaporation works. First, collect the necessary supplies to complete the experiment: one sheet of black construction paper, a small paint brush, a small cup of water, and a watch with a second hand. Next, place the paper on a dry, flat surface in the shade. Now wet the paint brush in the water and dab a drop of water onto the black paper. Immediately after wetting the paper, begin timing how long it takes for the water stain to dry up, or evaporate. When the water has dried, write the time down. At this point, begin the same experiment again by completing all of the steps, except that the paper should be placed under direct sunlight, or some type of heat source. Time how long the water takes to evaporate again. Finally, compare the two times, and answer the following questions: Where did the water go? Did a heat source, such as sunlight, make the water evaporate more slowly or more quickly? Why? By completing this simple experiment, it is possible to easily learn about the process of evaporation.

a. Underline the topic sentence and the concluding sentence of the paragraph.

b. List the steps for completing the experiment in the order you find them.

1. *Collect the necessary supplies to complete the experiment.*
2. ....
3. ....
4. ....
5. ....
6. ....
7. ....

c. How are the steps in the paragraph connected together? What words do you see that help show the sequence to follow? Underline them.

Connectors

What are connectors?

Connectors are words and phrases that help tie sentences together in a paragraph. They show the relationships between the ideas in a paragraph. They are not used between every sentence, but are used often enough to make the order clear. Here are some common connectors that show time order or the order of steps:

first, second, third, etc.	finally, at last	until
next	the last step	as
then	before, prior to	
after, after that	while	
now, at this point	when	

10 Choose appropriate connectors to connect the steps in this paragraph about preparing for a trip.

Planning a vacation abroad? Here are some suggestions to make your trip successful. [a] ...., find out if you need a visa for the country that you want to visit. Make sure you have enough time to apply for it [b] .... you buy your ticket. [c] .... you've found out about visas, you should research airfares and schedules. [d] ...., look for the best flight for you. Remember, the cheapest flight may stop over in several cities and reduce the amount of time you have to spend at your destination. You might want to fly direct. [e] .... you're researching flights, you can also ask your travel agent about getting a good deal on a hotel. It's a good idea to book your flight and hotel early if you're sure of your destination. If you haven't already done it, the [f] .... step is to learn about places to visit, the weather, the food, and other details about the country. The Internet can be a very useful source of information. [g] ...., on the day of your flight, make sure you go to the airport at least two hours before your flight. Now you are ready to start enjoying your vacation!

Ordering sentences

11 **Order the steps to form a process paragraph. Write 1 next to the first step, 2 for the second step, and so on.**

Introduction to linguistics: language-learning research project

Conduct an experiment to find out whether learners of English use English more correctly on a written test or in informal conversation.

a. .... Next, make a written test that checks the grammar point you are researching. This could be a fill-in-the-blanks test, a correct-the-errors test, or another style. It should have at least ten questions, but it should not be too long.

b. .... After giving the written test, interview each learner individually for about ten minutes. Try to make the interviews informal and friendly. Be sure to ask questions that will encourage learners to use the grammar point you are researching. Record the interviews. (Ask for learners' permission first!)

c. .... After you have counted the errors, calculate the score as a percentage. Do this for the written test and the spoken inteview.

d. .... Next, read the tests and listen to the recordings. Make a note of how many times your chosen grammar point was used, and how many times it was used incorrectly. Do this for both the written test and the recorded conversation.

e. .... Third, find about ten intermediate-level English learners who will agree to take your test. Arrange a time to give the test to each learner.

f. .... Finally, prepare two graphs to compare your results. Did learners make more mistakes on the written test or while they were speaking?

g. ..... First, choose a common English grammar point you would like to use in your research. Ask your teacher for a suggestion if you need help choosing one.

12 **Write a process paragraph about a topic that you know well. First, brainstorm all the steps that need to be followed. Then write the paragraph. Remember to use transitions.**

Review

13 **This paragraph describes a city park, but it doesn't have enough descriptive details. Imagine that you live next to a park. Rewrite the paragraph, adding description, to make it more interesting.**

I live next to a park. The park is large and has trees and grass. There is a lake in the park where you can see people enjoying many activities. There are many places to sit and relax. There are many paths that you can walk on, and everywhere you walk you can see flowers. I really enjoy spending time in this park.

5 Opinion Paragraphs

In this unit, you will learn how to ...

- **distinguish between fact and opinion.**
- **organize and write paragraphs expressing opinions and arguments.**
- **use transition words to express causality.**
- **use modal expressions to make recommendations.**

Facts and opinions

A *fact* is a piece of information that is true: *That movie was three hours long.*

An *opinion* is an idea or belief about a particular subject: *That movie was boring.*

Writers use facts to support their opinions and to show why they hold their beliefs.

An opinion paragraph

1 Read this letter to the editor of a newspaper. Answer the questions.

Dear Editor,

More people should ride bicycles into town. Last year, seventy-three percent of all workers drove their own car to work. Car traffic in town is terrible, parking places are hard to find, and pollution from cars is a real problem. Citizens who want a cleaner, nicer place to live ought to try this non-polluting form of transportation. Cycling is good exercise, too! The city must not allow this problem to get worse. Instead, people should ride bicycles to work and school—and enjoy the health benefits of daily exercise.

Bill Adams
Bellingham

a. What is the main idea of this paragraph? Circle the sentence.

b. What is the writer's purpose? Why did he write this letter?

c. Underline the sentences or parts of sentences that show an opinion.

d. Why do you think the writer included a fact in this paragraph?

2 **Do these types of writing use mostly facts, mostly opinions, or an even mixture of both? Write F for fact, O for opinion, or B for both. Explain your choices to a partner.**

a. .... movie review
b. .... advice column
c. .... police report of a crime
d. .... travel brochure
e. .... news report
f. .... book report for a college literature class
g. .... magazine advertisement
h. .... personal e-mail to a friend

3 **Can you think of other types of writing that use opinions? Make a list. Then make a list of types of writing that use facts.**

Use opinions ....

Use facts ....

4 **Read these sentences. Write F if the sentence is a fact, and O if the sentence is an opinion.**

a. .... Airfares have become too expensive.
b. .... English is an easier language to learn than Arabic.
c. .... Owls are birds that hunt at night.
d. .... I was born in New York City.
e. .... Exercise is the best way to stay healthy.
f. .... Internet use has increased every year since its beginning.
g. .... Engineering is the best career choice.
h. .... Big cities are dangerous at night.

5 **Write three fact sentences and three opinion sentences.**

a. ....
b. ....
c. ....
d. ....
e. ....
f. ....

6 **Share your sentences with a partner. Decide which of your partner's sentences are fact and which are opinion.**

Modal auxiliaries

➲ Using modal auxiliaries

When you speak, you introduce opinions with phrases like *I think*, *In my opinion*, and *I believe*. In general, these introductory phrases are not needed in writing. They can even make you sound less sure of your ideas. Instead, writers use grammatical methods such as modal auxiliary verbs to express their opinions. Modal auxiliary verbs show the strength of a writer's opinion or argument.

AFFIRMATIVE:

The city	could	add more bike paths.	weakest
	should		▼
	ought to		
	has to / must		strongest

NEGATIVE:

The city	doesn't have to	allow more cars.	weakest
	shouldn't		▼
	can't / must not		strongest

7 **Look again at the paragraph in exercise 1 on page 33. Circle the modal auxilaries. How strong do you think the writer's opinions were? Discuss with a partner.**

8 **Read the paragraph below. Circle the most appropriate modal auxiliary in each sentence.**

Dear Editor,

I agree with Bill Adams's opinion in his recent letter saying that people a. ***should / don't have*** to ride their bicycles into town. However, there is one problem with this idea. The roads in town are so narrow and full of cars that you b. ***can't / ought to*** ride safely on them. If people are going to ride bicycles into town, the city c. ***could / must*** make some bike paths for people to use. Maybe the city d. ***could / mustn't*** charge a small additional tax on fuel to pay for the bike paths. Motorists have created the problem, so motorists e. ***could / should*** pay for the solution. The city f. ***ought to / doesn't have to*** support cyclists like Bill Adams by building more bike paths.

Melissa Green
Parkville

Expressing opinions: class survey

9 **Read these statements that express opinions. Add three of your own.**

Name:	....	....	....
1. Grocery stores and shops shouldn't give plastic bags to customers.	☐ agree ☐ disagree	☐ agree ☐ disagree	☐ agree ☐ disagree
2. University students should not have part-time jobs.	☐ agree ☐ disagree	☐ agree ☐ disagree	☐ agree ☐ disagree
3.	☐ agree ☐ disagree	☐ agree ☐ disagree	☐ agree ☐ disagree
4.	☐ agree ☐ disagree	☐ agree ☐ disagree	☐ agree ☐ disagree
5.	☐ agree ☐ disagree	☐ agree ☐ disagree	☐ agree ☐ disagree

10 **Share your statements with three classmates. Say how you feel about your partners' statements by saying, "I agree" or "I disagree," and then adding one sentence. Check (✓) your partners' opinions about your statements.**

11 **Read the opinion paragraphs in exercise 1 on page 33 and exercise 8 on page 35 again. Then write a paragraph about one of the opinions you expressed in exercise 10 above. Brainstorm ideas, narrow your topic, and then write. Remember to use modal auxiliaries.**

2 Read the following paragraph and answer the questions.

a. What two things does the paragraph talk about?

b. Is the paragraph mostly comparing or contrasting? How do you know?

In recent years, new technology such as cellular telephones and the Internet have made life more convenient. Cellular telephones allow people to talk to one another almost anywhere. Likewise, the Internet gives people the ability to talk to one another very easily, even across countries. Second, cellular phones and the Internet are available 24 hours per day, so people can speak or connect at any time, day or night. Another convenient quality of these two types of technology is that they both allow people to find out information without even leaving one's home. A person can access the Internet through most types of cellular phones, and the Internet can be used to look up virtually any topic of interest. Clearly, cellular phones, the Internet, and other new types of technology that exist today provide a great deal of convenience for people.

Comparative and contrastive structures

➲ Using comparative structures

These words and phrases are used for writing comparisons:

and	*The man **and** the woman are tall.*
both	***Both** of the tables have broken legs.*
both … and	***Both** my neighbor **and** I are selling our cars.*
also	*The stores are closing for the holiday. The bank is **also** closing.*
too	*Kathy is planning to go to the party, and I am, **too**.*
neither … nor	***Neither** Joe **nor** Steve went to the meeting last night.*
similar to	*Their new computer is **similar to** the one my brother bought.*
the same as	*Is the restaurant where you had dinner **the same as** the place where I ate last month?*
(just) as + adjective + as.	*His coat is **just as warm as** the more expensive one.*
likewise	*My parents were born in a small village. **Likewise**, my brothers and I also grew up in a small town.*
similarly	*There are many parks to visit in that city. **Similarly**, there are several parks in my hometown, too.*

3 Complete these sentences with phrases from above.

a. .... cell phones .... computers will work without a power source.

b. To access the Internet on my laptop, I need to connect to a wireless signal. .... , my cell phone needs to connect to a network.

c. I pay a monthly fee for .... my cell phone and my Internet services.

➲ Using contrastive structures

These words and phrases are used for writing contrasts:

more / less + adjective / adverb + than	*Eating out is usually* ***more expensive than*** *cooking at home.*
adjective + er + than	*My bedroom is* ***bigger than*** *my sister's room.*
but, while, though	*I enjoy eating fruit for dessert,* ***but*** */* ***while*** */* ***though*** *my friend likes chocolate.*
not the same as	*This book* ***isn't the same as*** *the one you bought.*
not as ... as	*Some people feel that doing exercise* ***isn't as fun as*** *watching TV.*
different from	*That style of shirt is* ***different from*** *the styles most people wear.*
in contrast	*The lakes we swam in were very clean and beautiful.* ***In contrast****, the lakes in my country are polluted.*
however	*The new store sells its clothing at low prices.* ***However****, other stores have better quality clothing.*
on the other hand	*My boyfriend likes to play sports.* ***On the other hand****, I prefer to do yoga.*

4 Complete these sentences with phrases from above.

a. The climate in the northern region of my country is very .... the weather in the southern region.

b. In the north, there are four distinct seasons .... in the south of the country, the seasons are not that different.

c. The northern area has mountains and the temperatures in the winter are extremely cold; .... , the south is much more flat and has warm to hot temperatures throughout the year.

d. Heavy rains and high humidity in the summer are common in the south, ... the north has only moderate rainfall throughout the year and much lower humidity.

Similarities and differences

5 **Write eight sentences about these two cars. Write about four similarities and four differences.**

Comparison / contrast organization

➲ Two methods for organizing a comparison / contrast paragraph

Method 1: Block organization

First, write about supporting points for the first topic. Then compare or contrast those same points to the second topic. This type of organization could be outlined like this:

Topic sentence comparing / contrasting two topics (A & B)

Points of comparison / contrast about Topic A

Points of comparison / contrast about Topic B

Concluding sentence

Reading a story in a book is often very different from seeing it as a movie. When you read a story, you need to use your imagination. A book usually gives a lot of description about the people, places, and things in the story, so you can create pictures in your mind. In addition, the conversations between people are always written with details that describe how the people look or feel while they are talking. When you read, you use a lot of imagination to help "see" the characters in the story. However, when you see a movie, it is a different experience. When you watch a movie, you don't need to use your imagination. The pictures on the screen give all the details about the people, places, and things in the story. The conversations are spoken out loud, so you just listen and watch. The feelings of the people come through their faces, body movements, and voices. Although a book and a movie might tell the same story, reading a book and watching a movie are very different experiences.

Method 2: Point-by-point organization

Compare or contrast one point about the two topics, then a second point, then a third point, and so on. This type of organization could be outlined like this:

Topic sentence comparing or contrasting two topics (A & B)

First point of comparison / contrast (A1, B1)

Second point of comparison / contrast (A2, B2)

Third point of comparison / contrast (A3, B3)

Fourth point of comparison / contrast (A4, B4)

Fifth point of comparison / contrast (A5, B5)

Concluding sentence

Marilyn Monroe and Princess Diana lived at different times in different countries, but their lives had some surprising similarities. First of all, both women had a difficult childhood. Monroe spent many years without parents in an orphanage, and Diana's mother left the family when she was only six. Later in their lives, both women married famous men. Princess Diana married Prince Charles, and Marilyn Monroe married a famous baseball player and later a famous writer. They also had difficult marriages and eventually separated from their husbands. Another similarity between Marilyn Monroe and Princess Diana was that they were both very popular. Diana was called "The people's princess" because she was so friendly. Although Monroe was famously beautiful, she was well-liked because she seemed very innocent. However, although they both seemed to have very happy lives, both women actually had emotional problems and often felt sad and depressed. Monroe went through serious depression and had to go to a hospital for treatment. Likewise, Diana suffered from an eating problem and was depressed during parts of her marriage. A last similarity between Marilyn Monroe and Princess Diana was their deaths at an early age. In fact, they were both thirty-six years old when they died, Monroe in 1962 and Diana in 1997. Maybe their similar life circumstances and lifestyles explain why Princess Diana and Marilyn Monroe also had similar personalities.

6 **Read the two paragraphs above then answer the questions.**

a. Which paragraph mostly compares and which mostly contrasts?

b. Finish filling in the outlines on page 46 for each paragraph.

Block organization: Paragraph 1

Topic sentence: Reading a story in a book is often very different from seeing it as a movie.

Topic A—reading a book
Supporting points:

1. ....

2. ....

Topic B— ....
Supporting points:

1. ....

2. ....

Point-by-point organization: Paragraph 2

Topic sentence: Marilyn Monroe and Princess Diana lived at different times in different countries, but their lives had some surprising similarities.

First point of comparison—difficult childhood

A1: ....

B1: Princess Diana—mother left family

Second point of comparison— ....

A2: Princess Diana—married Prince Charles, later separated from him

B2: ....

Third point of comparison— ....

A3: ....

B3: ....

Fourth point of comparison—had emotional problems

A4: Marilyn Monroe— ....

B4: ....

Fifth point of comparison— ....

A5: ....

B5: ....

7 **Look again at the paragraph in exercise 2 on page 41. Does it use point-by-point or block organization? How do you know?**

8 **Read this list of details about two types of sports. Then make a list of similarities and a list of differences below. Discuss your answers with a partner.**

Team sports

- teach the skills needed for working with others
- individual strengths benefit the group's success
- players rely on each other and close relationships can develop
- coaches are important for managing the group's diverse talent and personalities
- individual talent may not be developed
- take time and practice to improve skills
- popular with fans

Individual sports

- teach the skills for working independently
- players rely on their own skills for success
- individual talent can be developed
- take time and practice to improve skills
- popular with fans
- a coach and player can develop a very close relationship

Similarities between the sports

....
....
....
....
....
....
....
....

Differences between the sports

....
....
....
....
....
....
....
....

9 **Write a comparison or contrast paragraph. Use either point-by-point organization or block organization.**

Advantages and disadvantages

➲ Writing about advantages and disadvantages

Another way to compare or contrast is to talk about *advantages* (positive points) or *disadvantages* (negative points) of a topic. If you are writing about one topic, it is usually best to discuss advantages and disadvantages in two separate paragraphs. If you are comparing or contrasting two topics, you could organize the paragraph in either point-by-point or block style.

10 Read this paragraph from a school newspaper. List the supporting points. Does the paragraph discuss advantages or disadvantages?

> Studying abroad and studying in your own country both have definite benefits for a student. Living in another country can be an exciting experience because everything seems new and different. The challenge of living in a new environment can give you courage and self-confidence, too. If you want to learn another language, living abroad is a great way to do that because you can read magazines or newspapers, watch television programs, or make friends with people who are native speakers. Another good reason to live abroad is to learn more about another culture. On the other hand, there are also advantages to staying in your own country to study. It is cheaper than living abroad, so you can save more money. Also, in your home country, everything is familiar. You don't need to worry about taking classes in a foreign language, and you can understand the culture and the expectations of teachers. Finally, if you stay in your own country, you can be close to your family and friends. So, if you are thinking about where to study, consider all of these benefits and make a decision that is right for you.

11 Write one or two paragraphs comparing or contrasting topics of your choice or one of these.

- the advantages and disadvantages of taking online / distance education courses
- living in a small town / living in a large city
- the advantages and disadvantages of having a job while in college
- using gas-powered vehicles / electric vehicles

Review

12 **List five words or phrases of comparison and five of contrast. Use them to compare and contrast two things in your college. Share your sentences with the rest of the class.**

Comparison	Contrast
....	....
....	....
....	....
....	....
....	....
....	....
....	....
....	....

13 **Work with a partner. Separate these ideas into advantages (A) and disadvantages (D).**

Studying English

a. .... takes a lot of time
b. .... classes are fun
c. .... grammar is difficult
d. .... useful for talking to people from other countries
e. .... good for using the Internet
f. .... lots of vocabulary to learn
g. .... too many tests to take
h. .... helps to understand English-language movies
i. .... my friends like English
j. .... pronunciation is difficult

14 **Now, in pairs, one person should write a paragraph about the advantages and the other person should write about the disadvantages of studying English. Add one new idea of your own to your paragraph.**

15 **Share your paragraphs with another pair of students.**

7 Problem / Solution Paragraphs

In this unit, you will ...

- **write about problems and solutions.**
- **use real conditionals.**
- **write a two-paragraph paper with linking phrases.**

➲ Problems and solutions

Problem / solution writing first explains a problem and then proposes one or more solutions to that problem. Often this type of writing requires more than one paragraph. In this unit, you will write a two-paragraph discussion of a problem and solution.

Problems and solutions

1 **Read the article from a website on page 51. What is the main idea of the first paragraph? What is the topic sentence?**

2 **Answer these questions.**

a. How is the first paragraph developed? What are the supporting ideas?

b. What do the supporting ideas show?

c. What is the main idea of the second paragraph? What is the topic sentence?

d. What solution does the writer offer? What details support or explain the solution?

e. Is there a concluding sentence in the first paragraph? In the second paragraph?

Writing about problems

➲ How to write a *problem paragraph*

A *problem paragraph* describes and discusses a problem issue. The topic sentence names the issue you will discuss. The supporting sentences show why this issue is a problem.

3 **Work with a partner or small group. Discuss why these issues are problems. Then add two more issues and discuss them.**

a. air pollution

b. traffic

c. overcrowded classrooms

d. ....

e. ....

Deforestation is a serious problem because forests and trees aren't just pretty to look at, they do an important job making the earth's environment suitable for life. They clean the air, store water, preserve soil, and provide homes for animals. They also supply food, fuel, wood products, and paper products for humans. In the past fifty years, more than half of the world's rain forests have been destroyed. Today, the forests of the world are being cut down at a rate of fifty acres every minute! Scientists say that if deforestation continues, the world's climate may change, floods may become more common, and animals will die.

One solution to the problem of deforestation is to use less paper. If you use less paper, fewer trees will be cut for paper making. How can you use less paper? One answer is to reduce your paper use by using both sides of the paper when you photocopy, write a letter, or write a paper for school. A second answer is to reuse old paper when you can, rather than using a new sheet of paper. The backs of old envelopes are perfect for shopping lists or phone messages, and when you write a rough draft of an essay, write it on the back of something else. A final answer is to recycle used paper products instead of throwing them away. Most schools, offices, and neighborhoods have some kind of recycling center. If you follow the three Rs—reduce, reuse, and recycle—you can help save the world's forests.

➲ Using conditional structures

The *real* (or *first*) conditional is a useful way to talk about both problems and solutions:

Fish ***will get*** *sick* ***if*** *factories* ***dump*** *their waste into streams.*

modal + main verb (will, can, could, should, etc.) — present

If *you* ***eat*** *fish from polluted waters, you* ***could get*** *sick too.*

present — modal + main verb (will, can, could, should, etc.)

Punctuation note: No comma is needed when the *if*-clause comes second:

People can become sick if they eat the sick fish.

The event in the *if*-clause is possible, or is likely to happen. The event in the result clause would logically follow. There are other types of conditional sentences, but real conditionals are the most common in writing about problems and solutions.

4 **Read the paragraphs on page 51 again. Underline the conditional sentences.**

5 **Complete these sentences by circling the correct form of the verb.**

a. It's difficult these days to be a university student. If you *want to* / *will want to* study full-time, it *costs* / *will cost* a lot of money.

b. If you *are* / *could be* in class all day, you *might not have* / *might have* enough time to get a part-time job.

c. If students *work* / *will work* part-time, it *could take* / *couldn't take* them more years to finish their studies because they are so busy.

d. If universities *don't stop* / *stop* increasing their tuition rates, only rich students *are* / *will be* able to study full-time.

e. We *must keep* / *mustn't keep* higher education affordable if we *want* / *will want* to have an educated population.

6 **Complete these sentences with your own ideas. Then compare with a partner.**

a. If it rains this weekend, ...

b. If the library isn't open tomorrow, ...

c. If gas prices increase even more, ...

d. .... , I will call you tonight.

e. .... , you can make a lot of money.

f. .... , I won't take a vacation.

7 **For each topic in exercise 3 on page 50, write one or two conditional sentences that explain the problem. Compare your sentences with a partner. Did you have similar or different ideas?**

8 **Choose one topic from exercise 3 on page 50. Brainstorm more ideas if necessary, then write a paragraph about it. Use conditional sentences.**

Linking problems with solutions

➲ How to link a solution paragraph to a problem paragraph

The first paragraph—the problem paragraph—explains the problem. The topic sentence of the second paragraph—the *solution paragraph*—introduces your solution or solutions. The supporting sentences show how your solution(s) will solve the problem. Use these phrases:

In order to solve these problems, …

To meet this need, …

One answer is …

A second / third / final answer is …

In order to overcome these problems, …

One solution is …

One thing we can do is …

9 **Read the solution paragraph on page 51 again. Circle the linking phrases.**

10 **Work with a group. For each of these topic sentences, brainstorm solutions. Introduce each solution with one of the phrases above. Then think of one more problem together, and give it to another group to discuss.**

a. We must reduce exam stress for high school students.

b. Teenagers spend so much time using their cell phones that they are no longer skilled at face-to-face interaction.

c. In the next five to ten years, experts predict that there won't be enough doctors and nurses to meet hospitals' needs.

d. We have to find ways to protect young children from violence on television.

e. ....

Writing solutions

➲ Finding the best solution

After you have brainstormed solutions to your problem, you need to select the best one or ones to write about in your solution paragraph. A strong solution clearly and reasonably solves the problem. A weak solution doesn't really solve the problem or is not practical or not logical.

11 **With a partner, talk about the solutions that this student brainstormed for her topic. Mark each one *strong*, *OK*, or *weak*.**

<u>Topic sentence:</u> *I need more spending money while I am in college.*

.... *borrow money from my friends*

.... *sell some of my things*

.... *ask my parents for money*

.... *play my guitar on the streets*

.... *get a part-time job*

.... *drop out of college and get a full-time job*

.... *buy lottery tickets*

.... *ride my bike to school instead of using public transportation*

.... *ask my professors for money*

.... *buy fewer CDs and new clothes*

12 **Use at least three solutions from the list in exercise 11 above to write a solution paragraph. Use linking phrases and conditional sentences to explain how the solutions will solve the problem. Share your paragraph with your partner.**

13 **For the problem paragraph you wrote in exercise 8 on page 53, brainstorm solutions. Edit your brainstorming, then write a solution paragraph. Use linking phrases and conditional sentences.**

Review

14 **Look at this list of ideas that a student brainstormed about his topic. Work with a partner to divide the ideas into problems and solutions. Try to add one more problem and solution to the list.**

Topic: getting along with a roommate

noisy roommate

make cleaning schedule

roommate is messy

argue about how to decorate room

fighting causes stress

set aside quiet time for studying

each person decorates half of the room

talk each week about concerns

problems

a. ....

b. ....

c. ....

d. ....

e. ....

solutions

f. ....

g. ....

h. ....

i. ....

j. ....

15 **Work alone. Use the ideas above to write a problem paragraph and a solution paragraph. Remember to write a topic sentence for each paragraph, and a concluding sentence for the solution paragraph. Use conditional sentences and linking phrases where you can. Then compare your paragraphs with your partner. What parts were similar? What parts were different?**

8 The Structure of an Essay

In this unit, you will learn ...

- **the definition of an essay.**
- **how to format an essay.**
- **how to write a thesis statement.**

➲ What is an essay?

An essay is a group of paragraphs written about a single topic and a central main idea. It must have at least three paragraphs, but a five-paragraph essay is a common assignment for academic writing.

The structure of an essay

➲ The three main parts of an essay

The introduction

This is the first paragraph of an essay. It explains the topic with general ideas. It also has a *thesis statement*. This is a sentence that gives the main idea. It usually comes at or near the end of the paragraph.

The body

These are the paragraphs that explain and support the thesis statement and come between the introduction and the conclusion. There must be one or more body paragraphs in an essay.

The conclusion

This is the last paragraph of an essay. It summarizes or restates the thesis and the supporting ideas of the essay.

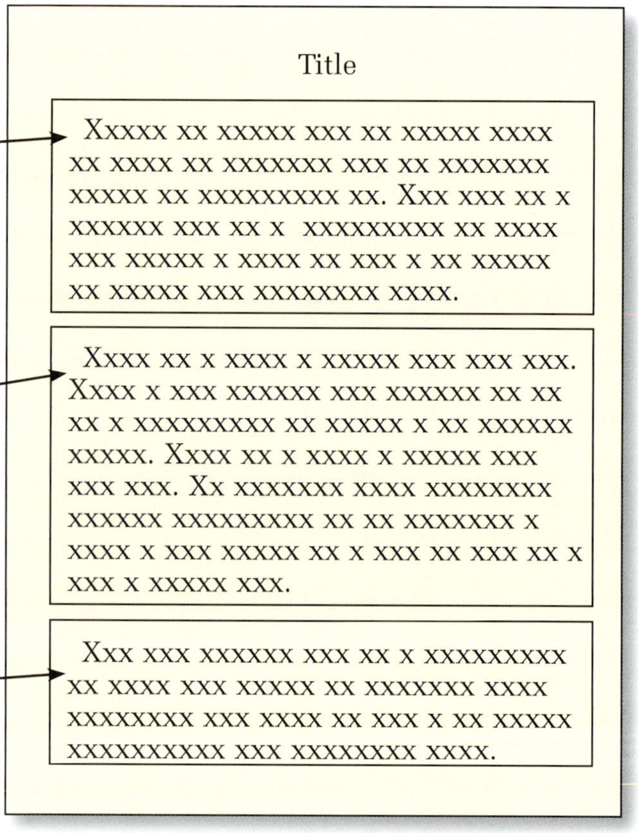

➲ How to format an essay

1. Use double spacing (leave a blank line between each line of writing).
2. Leave 2.5 centimeters (1 inch) of space on the sides, and the top and bottom of the page. This space is called the ***margin***.
3. If you type your essay, start the first line of each paragraph with five spaces (one tab). This is called ***indenting***. If you write by hand, indent about 2 centimeters (¾ inch).
4. Put the title of your essay at the top of the first page in the center.

Label the three parts of this essay: introduction, body paragraphs, and conclusion.

American and British English: One Language with Many Differences

The English language came to be the world language that it is today by events that happened hundreds of years ago. British colonization and trade led to the spread of the English language to many areas around the world, and by the early 1600's English was introduced to North America. Although the English used in the United States and the United Kingdom is generally mutually intelligible, it has developed several differences, including pronunciation, grammar, punctuation, and spelling. Certain differences in vocabulary and the use of idioms between American and British English can cause misunderstandings between speakers.

Vocabulary is one area where many differences can be found between American and British English. There are many examples of a particular vocabulary word having different meanings. Words such as *bill* (AmE = paper money or invoice, BrE = invoice), *biscuit* (AmE = slightly salty, thick pastry, BrE = sweet dessert, like an American cookie) and *football* (AmE = *soccer*) are three well-known examples. Other examples of vocabulary that are entirely different words for the same meaning include *elevator* (AmE) and *lift* (BrE); *gas* (AmE) and *petrol* (BrE); *period* (AmE) and *full stop* (BrE); *apartment* (AmE) and *flat* (BrE); *potato chips* (AmE) and *crisps* (BrE); *subway* (AmE) and *underground* (BrE); *line* (AmE) and *queue* (BrE); and *intersection* (AmE) and *crossroads* (BrE).

In addition to words, there are certain idioms, or phrases, that differ between the two forms of English. Most of the phrases differ by only one or two words and can sometimes cause misunderstandings between speakers of American and British English. Some examples include (BrE) *a drop in the ocean* and (AmE) *a drop in the bucket*, which mean "a small part of something that is much larger"; (BrE) *blow one's trumpet* and (AmE) *blow (or toot) one's horn,* which mean "to brag about one's own accomplishments"; and (BrE) *tuppence worth* and (AmE) *two cents' worth,* which mean "to offer one's opinion or advice." One phrase that can cause some confusion in conversation is *I don't mind.* If a person is asked whether he would like tea or coffee, for example, the BrE response "I don't mind" means that either choice is acceptable, while the AmE response would most likely be "I don't care."

The examples above are only a small sample of the various ways American English and British English differ. However, although vocabulary differences can cause some misunderstandings, generally speakers of both forms of English can understand one another with little difficulty. Differences between American and British English have developed over the centuries, and these differences will likely continue to develop and change into the future.

Thesis statements

➲ What is a thesis statement?

The *thesis statement* is the sentence that tells the main idea of the essay. It can be compared to a topic sentence, which gives the main idea of a paragraph. The thesis statement can express an opinion: *Travel is an effective way to bring people of different cultures together and learn about one another.* It can also state an argument or fact to be defended or explained: *There are several ways that technology has made classroom instruction more effective.* It usually comes at or near the end of the introductory paragraph.

2 **Look at the essay in exercise 1 on page 57 again. Underline the thesis statement.**

3 **In these introductory paragraphs, underline the thesis statement. Then circle the topic and draw another line under the main idea in each thesis statement. Share your answers with a partner.**

a.

The British eat many different kinds of food, but the typical diet of many people includes eating a lot of fast food and ready-made dishes. The popularity of hamburger and pizza restaurants has increased greatly over the years. As a result of this diet, many British people have food-related health problems. To create a healthier society, people should learn about eating a good diet and should teach their children to do the same.

b.

Everybody knows the koala, that cute Australian animal that resembles a teddy bear. Although koalas look like toys, they are actually strong climbers and spend their days in the treetops. Mother koalas carry their babies around from tree to tree in a pouch, or pocket, on their stomach. Although there were millions of koalas in Australia in the past, they are now a protected species of animal. As a result of human population growth, deforestation, and hunting, the number of koalas has declined.

c.

Taoism is an ancient philosophy from Asia that places great importance on the natural world. Taoists believe that spirit can be found in every person or thing, living or non-living. For the Taoist, even a mountain or a stone contains spirit. Lao Tsu, a Taoist writer and philosopher, said "People follow earth. Earth follows heaven. Heaven follows the Tao. The Tao follows what is natural." For thousands of years in China and other Asian countries, gardens have been an important way to create a place where people can feel the spirit of the natural world. Creating a Taoist garden is an art. No two Taoist gardens are exactly alike, but all Taoist gardens include four essential elements: water, mountains, buildings, and bridges.

➲ Writing a strong thesis statement

- A thesis statement gives the author's opinion or states an important idea about the topic. It should give an idea that can be discussed and explained with supporting ideas:

  The qualifications for entering a university in my country are unreasonable.

  When studying a second language, there are several ways to improve your use of the language.

  These are strong thesis statements. They can be discussed or explained.

- A thesis statement should not be a sentence that only gives a fact about the topic:

  In the Northern Hemisphere, the summer months are warmer than the winter months.

  This is not a strong thesis statement. It cannot be discussed or argued about.

- A thesis statement should not state two sides of an argument equally:

  There are advantages and disadvantages to using nuclear power.

  This could be a topic sentence, but it is not a thesis statement. It gives two sides of an argument without giving a clear opinion of support or disagreement. It could be revised like this:

  Although there are some advantages, using nuclear power has many disadvantages and should not be a part of our country's energy plan.

  This is a strong thesis statement. It clearly gives the writer's opinion about nuclear power.

4 Read these thesis statements below. Write ✓ (strong thesis statement), F (fact only—a weak thesis statement), or N (no clear opinion—a weak thesis statement).

a. .... The top government official in my country is the prime minister.

b. .... Many diseases are caused by both genetic and environmental factors.

c. .... India became an independent country in 1947.

d. .... To be a successful student, good study habits are more important than intelligence.

e. .... There are several advantages of owning a car, but there are also many disadvantages.

f. .... Half of the families in my country own a house.

g. .... Using public transportation would be one of the best ways to solve the traffic and pollution problems in cities around the world.

h. .... While traveling, staying in a hotel offers more comfort, but sleeping in a tent is less expensive.

i. .... Classical music concerts are very popular in my country.

j. .... In order to create a successful advertisement, it is necessary to consider three issues: who should be targeted, where the ad should be placed, and what type of ad should be made.

Writing thesis statements

➲ How to connect the thesis statement and the essay

The body paragraphs of an essay should always explain the thesis statement. In addition, each body paragraph should discuss *one* part of the thesis. Look at the following thesis statement. The topics to be discussed are underlined:

To create a successful advertisement, it is necessary for advertisers to answer three questions: What are we selling?, Who are we selling it to?, and How can we make people want to buy it?

Possible topic sentences for each body paragraph:

1. *The first step in creating a successful advertisement is to completely understand the product that is being sold and how it can be used.*
2. *A second important part of creating an advertisement is deciding who is expected to buy the product.*
3. *Finally, a way must be found to create an ad that will make people want to buy the product.*

5 **Look at the introductory paragraphs in exercise 3 on page 58. What should the body paragraphs discuss for each thesis statement? Write your ideas and then compare your answers with a partner.**

➲ How to develop a thesis statement

One way to develop a thesis statement for an essay is to write opinions you have about the topic. Begin, *I think that* … and complete the sentence with your opinion. Then remove *I think that* … and the remaining words make a possible thesis statement.

Topic: diet / food

~~*I think that*~~ *a vegetarian diet is one of the best ways to live a healthy life.*

~~*I think that*~~ *governments should restrict the use of chemicals in agriculture and food production.*

After you have written several opinion statements, choose the one that would make the best thesis. Remember to decide if the sentence gives a clear opinion, states a fact, or presents two sides without a clear argument.

6 **For each of these topics, write two or three opinions you have, starting with *I think that*.**

a. exercise

....

....

....

b. university study

....

....

....

c. the Internet

....

....

....

d. music

....

....

....

7 **Now cross out the *I think that* in the statements you wrote in exercise 6 on page 61. Choose the best thesis statement for each topic. Share these with a partner. Decide which ones are good thesis statements.**

8 **Choose one of your thesis statements from exercise 7 above. Circle the topics that must be explained in the essay. Write a topic sentence for each of the circled ideas.**

Review

9 **Complete the crossword.**

The topic sentence gives the [1.] m___ idea of a [2.] p___ . Likewise, the thesis statement gives the main [3.] i___ of an [4.] e___.

The [5.] s___ sentences of a paragraph explain the topic sentence, just as the [6.] b___ paragraphs of an essay explain the thesis statement.

The last sentence of a paragraph is called the [7.] c___ sentence, and the last paragraph of an essay is called the [8.] c___.

9 Outlining an Essay

In this unit, you will learn …

- **the purpose of an outline.**
- **how to write an outline.**

What is an outline?

An outline is a list of the information you will put in your essay. You can see an example of an outline on page 65.

An outline …

- begins with the essay's thesis statement.
- shows the organization of the essay.
- tells what ideas you will discuss and shows which ideas will come first, second, and so on.
- ends with the essay's conclusion.

Writing an outline before you write an essay will ...

- show you what to write before you actually begin writing.
- help make your essay well organized and clearly focused.
- keep you from forgetting any important points.

Imagine your skeleton: although you don't see it, it supports your body. In the same way, although a reader won't see your outline, making an outline in advance will support your essay by providing its structure. In fact, adding more information to an outline is called "fleshing it out."

Looking at an outline

1 Read the outline on page 65. Answer the questions.

a. What will be the thesis statement of the essay?

b. How many body paragraphs will the essay have?

c. How many supporting points will the third paragraph have? What will they be?

d. How many details will the fourth paragraph have? What will they be?

Writing an outline

➲ How to write an outline

Before writing an outline, you must go through the usual process of gathering ideas, editing them, and deciding on a topic for your writing. Writing an outline can be a very useful way of organizing your ideas and seeing how they will work together.

To show how the ideas work together, number them. To avoid confusion, use several different types of numbers and letters to show the organization of the ideas. Use roman numerals (I, II, III, IV, V, VI, etc.) for your essay's main ideas: your introduction and thesis statement, your body paragraphs, and your conclusion. Write all of these first, before going into more detail anywhere.

I. Introduction
II. First main idea
III. Second main idea
IV. Third main idea
V. Conclusion

Next, fill in more information for your body paragraphs by using capital roman letters (A, B, C, etc.). Use one letter for each supporting idea in your body paragraph. Complete this information for each body paragraph before going into more detail.

I. Introduction
II. First main idea
    A. First supporting point
    B. Second supporting point
    … and so on.

Finally, use Arabic numerals (1, 2, 3, etc.) to give details for your supporting points. Not every supporting point will have details, and some points will have several. It is not important to have the same number of details for every supporting point.

I. Introduction
II. First main idea
    A. First supporting point
        1. First detail
        2. Second detail
    B. Second supporting point
        1. First detail
        2. Second detail
        … and so on.

Don't Support Nuclear Energy!

I. Nuclear power is not a good energy source for the world.

II. Very expensive

A. Nuclear fuel is expensive

B. Nuclear power plants are expensive to build and operate

1. Cost of construction
2. Cost of training workers
3. Cost of safety features

III. Nuclear materials are not safe

A. Nuclear fuels are dangerous

1. Mining fuels produces radioactive gas
2. Working with radioactive fuels can harm workers

B. Nuclear waste products are dangerous

1. Very radioactive
2. Difficult to dispose of or store safely

IV. There is a possibility of disastrous accidents

A. Nuclear power plants can fail

1. Three Mile Island, U.S.A. (1979)
2. Darlington, Canada (1992)
3. Sellafield, England (2005)

B. Workers can make mistakes

1. Chernobyl, U.S.S.R. (1986)
2. Tokaimura, Japan (1999)
3. Asco, Spain (2007–2008)

C. Natural disasters can occur

1. Tornado: Mururoa, the Pacific (1981)
2. Earthquake: Fukushima, Japan (2011)

V. Because of the cost and the danger, the world should develop different types of energy to replace nuclear power.

2 **Fill in this outline for the essay in Unit 8, exercise 1 on page 57. Then compare with a partner.**

The differences between American and British English.

I. Thesis statement: ....

II. Vocabulary differences

A. ....

1. bill

2. ....

3. ....

B. Different words with same meaning

1. elevator/lift

2. gas/..

3. period/..

4. ....

III. ....

A. a drop in the ocean/bucket

B. ....

C. ....

D. ....

IV. Conclusion: ....

....

....

....

3 **Label each statement T for thesis statement, M for main idea, S for supporting point, or C for conclusion.**

Title: The Benefits of Yoga

a. .... Develops clear thinking
b. .... Physical benefits
c. .... Improves concentration
d. .... Reduces fear, anger, and worry
e. .... Mental benefits
f. .... Improves blood circulation
g. .... Improves digestion
h. .... Helps you feel calm and peaceful
i. .... Develops self-confidence
j. .... Practicing yoga regularly can be good for your mind, your body, and your emotions.
k. .... Makes you strong and flexible
l. .... Therefore, to build mental, physical, and emotional health, consider practicing yoga.
m. .... Emotional benefits

4 **Arrange the ideas in exercise 3 above into an outline. Compare your finished outline with a partner.**

I. ....

II. ....

A. ....

B. ....

III. ....

A. ....

B. ....

C. ....

IV. ....

A. ....

B. ....

C. ....

V. ....

Evaluating an outline

➲ The outline checklist

Before you start writing your essay, check your outline for organization, support, and topic development. If possible, have a friend or your instructor check your outline too.

Organization

❑ paragraphs in the right order
❑ supporting points and details in the right order

Support

❑ each main idea related to the thesis statement
❑ each supporting point related to the paragraph's main idea
❑ each detail related to the paragraph's supporting points

Topic development

❑ enough (and not too many) main ideas to develop the thesis statement
❑ enough (and not too many) supporting points for each main point
❑ enough (and not too many) details for each supporting point

5 **With a partner, check the outline on page 69 for organization, support, and topic development. What should the author add, subtract, or change in this outline? Share your ideas with another pair. Did you make the same recommendations?**

In 1848, gold was discovered in California. People from all over the world rushed to California to look for gold—they wanted to become rich. This was called "the gold rush."

The Effects of the California Gold Rush on the City of San Francisco

I. The California gold rush changed San Francisco in ways that we can still see today.

II. History of the gold rush
   A. 1848
      1. Gold was discovered near San Francisco
      2. The U.S. president tells the country there's gold in California
   B. 1864: the gold rush ends
   C. 1849: the gold rush begins as people from all over the world go to California to look for gold. Gold is very easy to find.
   D. 1850s: gold becomes more difficult to find; big, expensive machines are now needed to find gold
   E. Gold rushes in other countries
      1. Australia (1851–53)
      2. South Africa (1884)
      3. Canada (1897–98)

III. Effects on San Francisco today
   A. People still come to San Francisco hoping to get rich
      1. Computer industry
   B. Sightseeing is very popular in San Francisco
   C. San Francisco is still an expensive city
      1. Houses and land
      2. Food & clothing
      3. Many new fast-food restaurants sell cheap hamburgers
   D. Still problems in the city
   E. Technological development is still important
   F. There is no gold mining today
   G. Character of San Francisco today

IV. Changes in California in the 1800s
   A. Population increased—more than 40,000 people moved to California in 1848–50
   B. Everything became more expensive
      1. Houses and land
   C. Problems with crime and violence
   D. Technology to find gold improved

V. The special personality of San Francisco can be traced in part to the famous gold rush of the 1800s.

6 Look at the thesis statement and topic sentences you wrote in Unit 8, exercise 8 on page 62. Write an outline for your essay. Then write the essay.

7 Exchange the essay you wrote for exercise 6 above with a partner. As you read your partner's essay, write an outline of the main ideas, supporting points, and details. Your partner will outline your essay. Discuss the outlines.

Review

8 Write a simple outline of yourself or your life. First, outline only the body paragraphs. Your main ideas could include physical characteristics, your personality, your habits, your family, places you have lived, jobs you have had, things you like and dislike, and so on.

9 Explain your outline to a partner. Your partner will then add a thesis statement and concluding statement.

10 Join another pair and present your complete outlines.

10 *Introductions and Conclusions*

In this unit, you will learn about ...

- **the purpose of an introduction.**
- **types of information in introductions.**
- **the purpose of a conclusion.**
- **techniques for writing conclusions.**

The importance of introductions and conclusions

Unit 8 explained that the introduction and the conclusion are two of the three main parts of an essay. Without an introduction and a conclusion, an essay is just a group of paragraphs. The introduction and the conclusion work together to make the topic and main ideas of the essay clear to the reader.

The introduction

What is an introduction?

The first paragraph of an essay, as you learned in Unit 8, is called the introduction. The introduction ...

- is usually five to ten sentences.
- catches the reader's interest.
- gives the general topic of the essay.
- gives background information about the topic.
- states the main point (the thesis statement) of the essay.

The introduction is often organized by giving the most general ideas first and then leading to the most specific idea, which is the thesis statement, like this:

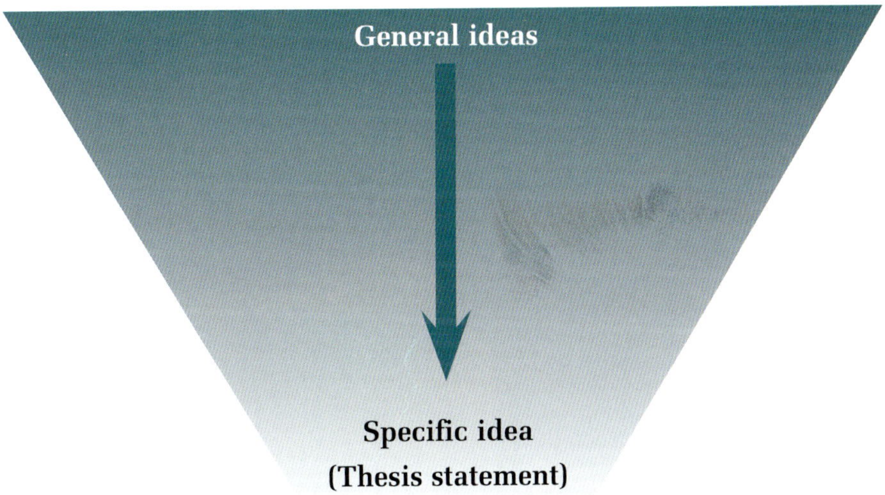

1 **Read the introduction to the essay in Unit 8, exercise 1 on page 57. Complete this diagram.**

General ideas:

English as a world language today is the result of events that happened a long time ago.

....

....

Specific idea (Thesis statement):

....

....

➲ How to write a strong introduction

A strong introduction …

- introduces the topic clearly.
- gives several sentences of information about the topic.
- states the thesis (the main idea) of the essay.

Any of the following will make an introduction weak:

- It doesn't give enough information about the topic or gives too much information about it.
- It talks about too many different topics.
- It does not state a clear thesis.

2 **Read and discuss the following introductions with a partner. Mark the strong introductions with a check (✓). Mark the weak introductions with an ✗. What could the writers do to make the weak introductions strong?**

a. ☐

The rate of babies being born in Japan and Korea has greatly decreased in the last fifty years. The decrease in number has caused several social changes.

b. ☐

The number of businesses using the Internet for selling products has increased greatly in recent years. Shoppers, too, are using the Internet in greater numbers to buy all types of products, such as books, cameras, and clothing. Although e-business has become popular, there are certain risks involved in Internet shopping that are a concern for both businesses and consumers.

c.

Stargazing—looking at the stars—is something everyone should try. I love it. When looking at the night sky, most people observe that the moon, planets, and stars move from the east side of the sky to the west over a period of several hours. In fact, this movement is actually the movement of the Earth rotating on its axis. In addition, as the Earth revolves around the sun throughout the year, different stars are visible at different times.

d.

The origins of Irish music can be traced back nearly 2,000 years to the time when the Celts arrived in Ireland. Music thrived under the rule of the Chieftans, but later declined during the British colonisation of Ireland. However, during the Great Famine of the 1840s, thousands of Irish people emigrated to North America in search of a better life, taking their music with them. Irish music soon became established in American cities with a high proportion of Irish immigrants, such as Chicago and Boston. These cities are popular tourist destinations with many interesting sights. However, Irish music really became well known to a wider audience in the 1970s, when musicians experimented with more modern arrangements of traditional songs and fusion with rock, world music and jazz. Jazz originated in the American South in the early twentieth century. Now, in the twenty-first century, Irish music is more popular and successful than ever.

e.

Adjusting to another culture's food can be a challenge for many travelers. The geography of a country can greatly affect the typical foods that are eaten by its people.

Types of information

➲ How to make an introduction interesting

To make an introductory paragraph interesting for the reader, you can include …

- interesting facts or statistics.
- a personal story or example.
- an interesting quotation.

3 **Read the three introductions in Unit 8, exercise 3 on page 58 again. What types of information does each introductory paragraph contain?**

4 **Look at the introduction of the essay you wrote for Unit 9, exercise 6 on page 70. With a partner, rewrite the introduction, making changes to improve it.**

The conclusion

➲ The importance of a conclusion

The conclusion is the final paragraph of the essay. A good concluding paragraph …

- summarizes the main points of the essay.
- restates the thesis (using different words).
- makes a final comment about the essay's main idea.
- may emphasize an action that you would like the reader to take.

Don't introduce new ideas in a conclusion. A conclusion only restates or gives further commentary on ideas discussed in the essay.

5 **Look at the essay in Unit 8, exercise 1 on page 57 again. Answer these questions.**

a. Does the conclusion use any of the four techniques described above? Which ones?

....

....

b. Which sentence in the conclusion restates the thesis (from the introduction)?

....

....

6 Match each of these introduction thesis statements with its rewritten version for a conclusion.

a. ...... A lack of adequate sleep can have several negative effects on a person's health and daily life.

b. ...... Traveling is a valuable learning experience for people, especially children and young adults.

c. ...... Learning to play a musical instrument is very beneficial for children.

d. ...... Creating and owning a business offers more advantages than working as an employee in a company.

e. ...... More houses should be adapted to use solar energy because it is clean and renewable.

f. ...... The Internet can be very useful for research, but it also contains a lot of incorrect information.

1. Young people can learn many things by traveling to other countries.

2. Despite the challenges, being an entrepreneur can offer more benefits than other types of employment.

3. Sleep deprivation can result in many harmful effects on the body including chronic tiredness, being unable to think clearly or remember things well, feeling depressed, and getting sick more easily due to a weakened immune system; clearly, getting enough sleep is an essential part of a healthy lifestyle.

4. The Internet gives access to a huge amount of knowledge, but users shouldn't believe everything they read there.

5. When children are exposed to music and are taught to play instruments such as the piano or violin, there are many positive effects.

6. The sun gives a constant, free supply of clean energy, which more homes should take advantage of.

7 **Read paragraph a in Unit 8, exercise 3 on page 58 again. Choose the best concluding paragraph, below.**

a.

Thanks to this publicity, the majority of people are now aware of what makes a good diet and they understand the related health benefits. Yet many still lack confidence in their ability to achieve healthy eating in their daily lives. The message to get across, especially to families and children, is that a healthy diet does not need to be expensive or difficult. Food that is bought freshly and prepared simply can be just as cheap and quick as a microwave dinner, and is certainly more delicious.

b.

Clearly, it is difficult to say that there is one type of British food. Every part of the country has its own special dishes based on the produce and tastes of that region. From the Ancient Britons and the Roman, Saxon and Viking invasions to present-day immigrants, the cuisine of the UK continues to change with its changing population.

c.

People who have come from other countries to live in the UK have brought their own traditions and customs with them and added them to British culture. It is possible to find restaurants from all different ethnic backgrounds, especially in larger cities around the country. Immigrants may also maintain their traditions by building places to practice their religion, such as mosques, temples, and churches. By continuing to follow some of their customs and beliefs, immigrants can remain in touch with their past while also living a new life in a new country.

8 **Look at the conclusion of the essay you wrote for Unit 9, exercise 6 on page 70. With a partner, rewrite the conclusion, making changes to improve it.**

Review

9 Complete the crossword puzzle.

A strong introduction catches the reader's [1] i___. It can do this by including interesting [2] f___, a personal [3] s___, or an interesting [4] q___. It also gives the general [5] t___ of the essay, several sentences of [6] i___ about the topic, and states the [7] t___.

A conclusion [8] s___ the main points of the essay. It also [9] r___ the thesis, makes a final [10] c___ about the essay's main idea, and it may emphasize an [11] a___ for the reader to take.

10 Write an introduction and conclusion for the outline you created for Unit 9, exercise 8 on page 70. Then exchange these with a partner. Make comments on your partner's paragraphs using the information you learned in this unit about writing good introductions and conclusions.

11 Unity and Coherence

In this unit, you will learn ...

- **the importance of unity in essay writing.**
- **how to edit an essay for unity.**
- **the importance of coherence in essay writing.**
- **methods of creating coherence.**

Writing effective essays

You've already learned that an essay should be organized into an introduction, a body, and a conclusion. The next step is to make sure that all three parts of the essay work together to explain your topic clearly.

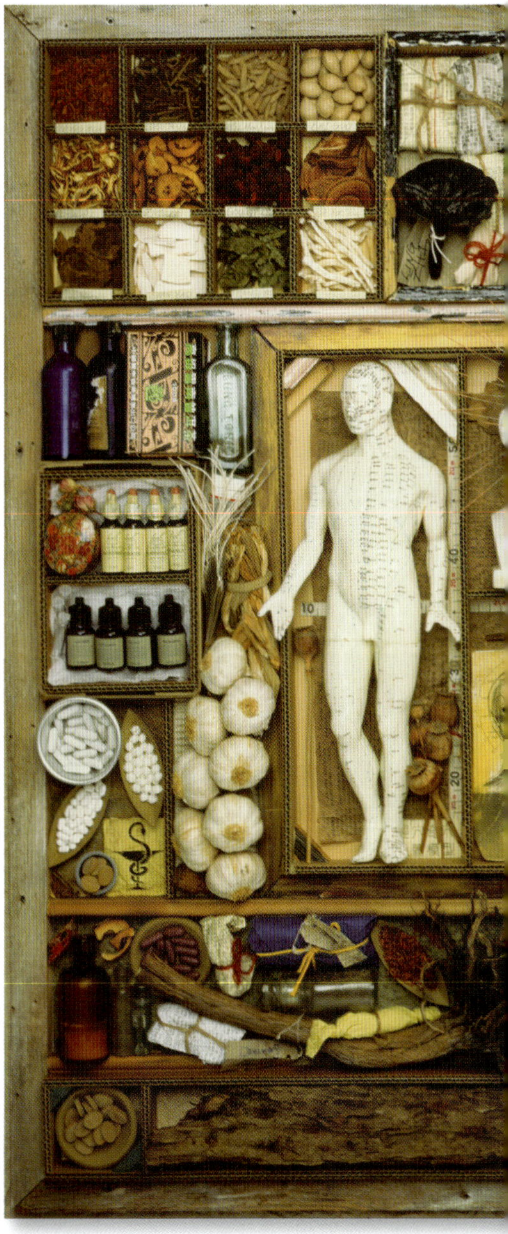

Unity in writing

What is unity?

Unity in writing is the connection of all ideas to a single topic. In an essay, all ideas should relate to the thesis statement, and the supporting ideas in a body paragraph should relate to the topic sentence.

1 Read the essay on page 79 about Chinese medicine. Then do these tasks.

a. Underline the thesis statement with two lines.

b. Underline each topic sentence with one line.

c. List the supporting ideas in each body paragraph on a separate piece of paper.

d. After you have finished, review the topic sentences and supporting ideas. With a partner, discuss how the topic sentences relate to the thesis statement and how the supporting sentences relate to the topic sentences. Is the essay unified?

Next Time, Try Chinese Medicine

The last time I had a cold, a friend suggested that instead of taking the usual cold medicines, I visit the traditional Chinese doctor in our city. Although I knew nothing about Chinese medicine, I decided to try it. When I walked in to the Chinese doctor's office, I was amazed. It was not at all like my usual doctor's. There were shelves up to the ceiling full of glass containers filled with hundreds of different dried plants and other things I could not identify. Could this really be a doctor's office? It seemed very strange to me. When I met the doctor, he explained that Chinese medicine is thousands of years old. The plants in the jars in his office were herbs. These herbs could be mixed together to make medicines. He explained the philosophy of Chinese medicine. The philosophy of traditional Chinese medicine is not the same as the philosophy of modern medicine, but it is useful for curing many health problems.

Modern medicine focuses on illness. If a patient with a cough visits a modern doctor, then the doctor will give the patient a medicine to stop the cough. If the patient also has a fever, the doctor may give a different medicine to stop the fever. For every person with a cough, the doctor will probably recommend the same cough medicine. The philosophy of modern medicine is to stop problems like coughing and fever as quickly as possible. Western doctors usually see illness as an enemy. They use medicines like weapons to fight diseases.

Chinese medicine, in contrast, has a different philosophy. Instead of focusing on a patient's health problems, Chinese medicine tries to make the patient's whole body well again. Specifically, doctors of Chinese medicine believe that inside people, there are two types of energy. The first type of energy, called "yin," is quiet and passive. The other type of energy, called "yang," is active. When these two energies are in equal balance, a person is healthy. When there is an imbalance—too much yin, for example—a person becomes unhealthy. A doctor of Chinese medicine doesn't try to stop a person's cough by giving a cough medicine. Instead, the doctor gives a mixture of herbs that will restore balance in the patient's body. As a result, when the body is in balance, the cough will stop naturally.

The Chinese doctor's herbs seemed strange to me at first, but they made me feel better. My cold wasn't cured instantly, but I felt healthy again after a few days. For a very serious health problem, I would probably visit a modern hospital, but the next time I catch a cold, I am going back to the Chinese doctor. Chinese medicine definitely works for some health problems.

Editing an essay for unity

➲ Keeping unity in an essay

One way to keep unity in an essay is to edit the outline for ideas that are not relevant to the thesis statement or topic sentences, as you learned in Unit 9. Likewise, after you have written the essay, it is helpful to review the text and look for ideas that do not relate to the thesis or the topic sentences.

2 **Read this thesis statement and body paragraphs. The writer has begun to cross out sentences that do not belong. There is still one large piece of the text that should be removed because it isn't relevant to the thesis. Can you find it? Compare your answer with a partner. Then look at the edited version in exercise 6 on page 85.**

Thesis statement: Sign language, the language used by many deaf people, has a 500-year history.

The first sign language for deaf people was developed in Europe in the 1500s. In Spain, a man named Pedro de Ponce was the first person to teach deaf children using sign language. Another Spaniard, Juan Pablo de Bonet, was the first person to write a book on teaching sign language to deaf people. ~~Most of his students were from rich families.~~ Another important teacher who influenced the development of sign language was a Frenchman named Abbé de L'Epée. L'Epée understood that deaf people could communicate without speech. He started to learn the signs used by a group of deaf people in Paris. Using these signs, he developed a more complete French sign language. ~~L'Epée also taught religion classes.~~ Another Frenchman, Louis Braille, also lived during this time. He invented a system of reading and writing for blind people, using raised bumps that can be felt with the fingers. In Germany, a man named Samuel Heinicke was another important teacher of the deaf during this time. However, he did not use sign language for instruction. Instead, he preferred to teach the deaf to understand other people by looking carefully at other people's mouths when they spoke. This is called lip or speech reading.

Speech reading became a popular way of teaching the deaf in the United States in the mid-1800s. Alexander Graham Bell, who invented the telephone, was one of the strongest supporters of teaching deaf people to do speech reading. Bell became interested in deafness and teaching deaf people. With his interest in science and the production of sound, he focused on ways of helping the deaf

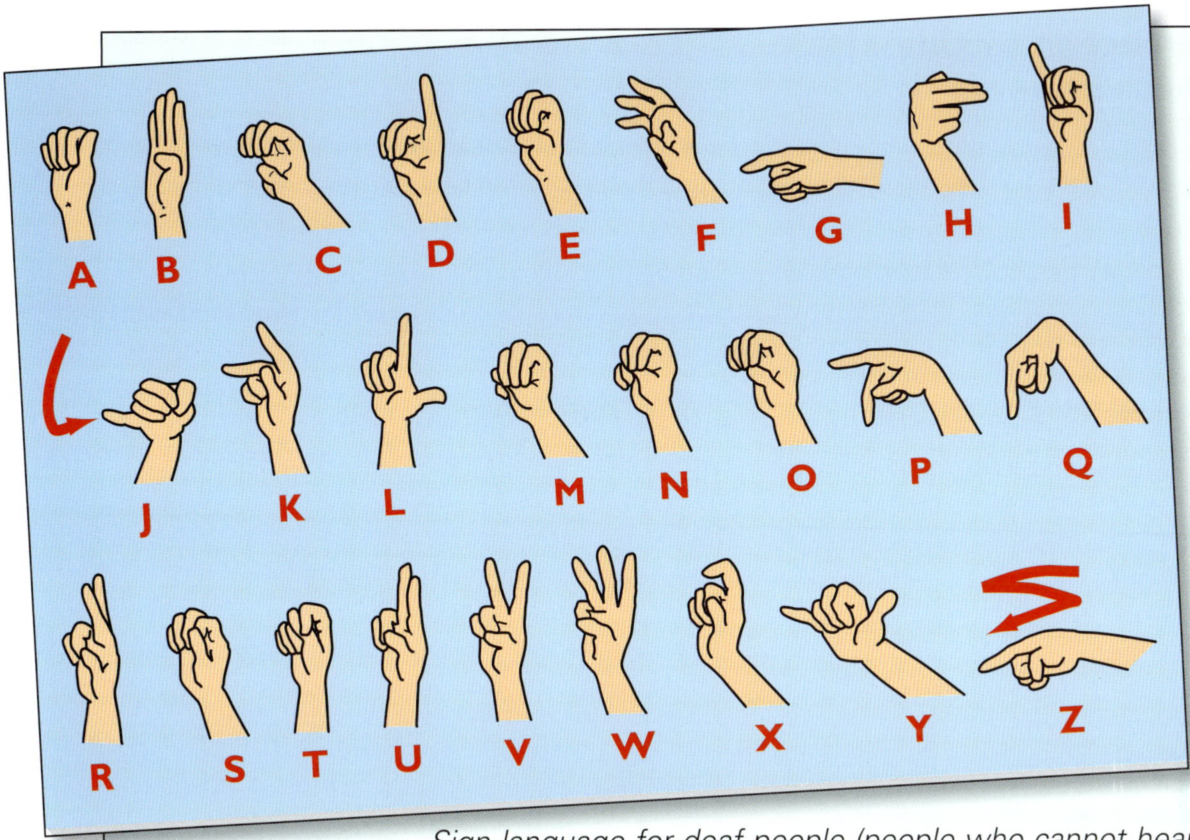

Sign language for deaf people (people who cannot hear)

communicate with listening tools and speech reading. He eventually opened a training school for teachers of the deaf.

~~Not much is known about the use of sign language among deaf people in the United States before the 1800's.~~ The early 1800s were an important period in the development of American Sign Language. In 1815, a man named Thomas Gallaudet became interested in teaching deaf people. He traveled to Europe to study ways of communicating with deaf people. He was twenty-seven years old at this time, and he studied at a school for deaf students in Paris for several months. In 1817, Gallaudet returned to the United States, and he brought with him Laurent Clerc, a deaf sign language teacher from Paris. Gallaudet started the first school for the deaf, and Clerc became the first sign language teacher in the U.S. ~~The school, called American School for the Deaf, still exists in Hartford, Connecticut.~~ American Sign Language developed from the mixture of signs used by deaf Americans and French Sign Language. Today, it is used by more than 500,000 deaf people in the United States and Canada. ~~About twenty million people in the United States have hearing problems, and about two million of these are deaf.~~

Coherence in writing

➲ What is coherence?

Coherence is related to unity. Ideas that are arranged in a clear and logical way are coherent. When a text is unified and coherent, the reader can easily understand the main points.

As you learned in Unit 9, creating an outline helps make a well-organized essay. When organizing your ideas, think about what type of organization is the best for your topic or essay type. Here are some examples of types of writing and good ways to organize them.

Type of writing	Type of organization
Chronology (historical events, personal narratives, processes)	Order by time or order of events / steps
Description	Order by position, size, and shape of things
Classification	Group ideas and explain them in a logical order
Comparison / contrast	Organize in point-by-point or block style
Argumentation / persuasion and cause / effect	Order from least important to most important

3 **Look again at the essay in exercise 1 on page 79. What type of organizational pattern does the essay use? How do you know? What about the text in exercise 2 on pages 80 and 81?**

Cohesive devices

➲ What is a cohesive device?

Cohesive devices are words and phrases that connect sentences and paragraphs together, creating a smooth flow of ideas. In this unit, we'll look at connectors, pronoun references, and repetition of key ideas.

Connectors

As you've learned in previous units, there are many connecting words and phrases in English that are used to connect sentences together or relate ideas to one another. Here are several types of writing and some common connectors that are used with them.

Chronology	Comparison	Contrast	Additional information	Examples	Cause and effect	Concluding ideas
before	*likewise*	*however*	*and*	*for example*	*therefore*	*in conclusion*
after	*compared to*	*on the other hand*	*also*	*in general*	*so*	*in summary*
next	*similarly*	*but*	*in addition*	*generally*	*thus*	*finally*
since	*as … as*	*yet*	*in fact*	*for instance*	*as a result*	*therefore*
first, second	*and*	*in spite of*	*furthermore*	*specifically*	*since*	*to conclude*
while		*in contrast*	*moreover*	*in particular*	*because*	*to summarize*
when		*although*	*Another … is/was*			
		instead				

4 Use connectors from the list above, or others that you know, to connect these sentences taken from the essay about Chinese medicine on page 79. When you have finished, compare your answers with the essay.

1. .... of focusing on a patient's health problems, Chinese medicine tries to make the patient's whole body well again. 2. .... , doctors of Chinese medicine believe that inside people, there are two types of energy. The first type of energy, called "yin," is quiet and passive. The other type of energy, called "yang," is active. … When there is an imbalance—too much yin, 3. .... —a person becomes unhealthy. A doctor of Chinese medicine doesn't try to stop a person's cough by giving a cough medicine. 4. .... , the doctor gives a mixture of herbs that will restore balance in the patient's body. 5. .... , when the body is in balance, the cough will stop naturally.

Pronoun reference

Two sentences can be connected by the use of a pronoun. A pronoun (*he, she, it, they,* etc.) takes the place of a noun (a person, place, thing, or idea) or a noun phrase (several words that refer to a person, place, thing, or idea). Look at the following example taken from the essay on sign language:

American Sign Language *developed from the mixture of signs used by deaf Americans and French Sign Language. Today,* it *is used by more than 500,000 deaf people in the United States and Canada.*

The pronoun *it* refers back to the subject, *American Sign Language*, and connects the two sentences together.

5 **For each of the *italicized* pronouns in this passage, identify the noun or noun phrase to which it refers. Write your answers on the lines below the text.**

Montreal, one of Canada's largest cities, is a popular tourist destination for several reasons. First, the city has a beautiful location. [a] ***It*** sits on an island in the middle of the St. Lawrence River. In addition, Montreal is both modern and historic. There are many luxury hotels, [b] ***it*** has a clean and efficient subway system, and visitors can find a wide variety of shops and restaurants, especially downtown. The oldest area of the town, the Vieux Montreal, is very beautiful because many of [c] ***its*** oldest buildings were protected as areas of the city were rebuilt or developed. The most interesting thing about Montreal may be [d] ***its*** French quality. Approximately two-thirds of the people living in or near Montreal are of French origin, and [e] ***they*** speak French as well as English. In addition to the strong French influence, there are large groups of people from Germany, Greece, Italy, Hungary, the West Indies, and China living [f] ***there***. All of [g] ***this*** makes Montreal a great place to visit.

a. it = ...

b. it = ...

c. its = ...

d. its = ...

e. they = ...

f. there = ...

g. this = ...

➲ Repetition of key nouns or ideas

Another way to connect ideas in an essay is by repeating important words and phrases. This will help the reader remember the main ideas in the text.

Modern **medicine** *focuses on illness. If a patient with a* <u>*cough*</u> *visits a modern doctor, then the doctor will give the patient a* **medicine** *to stop the* <u>*cough*</u>*. If the patient also has a fever, the doctor may give a different* **medicine** *to stop the fever. For every person with a* <u>*cough*</u>*, the doctor will probably recommend the same* <u>*cough*</u> **medicine***. The philosophy of modern* **medicine** *is to stop problems like* <u>*coughing*</u> *and fever as quickly as possible.*

6 Read these revised paragraphs from the essay on sign language. Underline examples of connector use, pronoun reference, and repetition of key words. Then compare your answers with a partner.

<u>Thesis statement:</u> Sign language, the language used by many deaf people, has a five-hundred-year history.

The first sign language for deaf people was developed in Europe in the 1500s. Three men in particular contributed a lot to the development of sign language. In Spain, a man named Pedro de Ponce was the first person to teach deaf children using sign language. In addition, another Spaniard, Juan Pablo de Bonet, wrote the first book on teaching sign language to deaf people, at about the same time. Another important teacher who influenced the development of sign language was a Frenchman named Abbé de L'Epée. L'Epée understood that deaf people could communicate without speech. He started to learn the signs used by a group of deaf people in Paris. Using these signs, he developed a more complete French sign language.

The early 1800s were an important period in the development of American Sign Language. In 1815, a man named Thomas Gallaudet became interested in teaching deaf people, so he traveled to Europe to study ways of communicating with deaf people. He was twenty-seven years old at this time, and he studied at a school for deaf students in Paris for several months. After that, Gallaudet returned to the United States, and he brought with him Laurent Clerc, a deaf sign language teacher from Paris. As a result of his experience in Europe, Gallaudet started the first school for the deaf, and Clerc became the first sign language teacher in the U.S. American Sign Language developed from the mixture of signs used by deaf Americans and French Sign Language. Today, it is used by more than 500,000 deaf people in the United States and Canada.

7 **This paragraph needs more connection. Revise it. Then share your version with other classmates.**

Ho Chi Minh City, in Vietnam, is a fascinating destination for travelers to Southeast Asia. It is located on the Mekong River. It was once an important trading center for the French in Southeast Asia. The influence of French culture can still be felt. Many people, especially the older generations, learned French in school and still can speak it very well. Some cafés serve French-style bread and pastries in Ho Chi Minh City. Expensive hotels and restaurants serve French food. Many of the buildings in the city are built in French style. The Vietnamese and the French fought. The French eventually left the country. There are museums and monuments documenting the country's long—and often bloody—history. If you are looking for a unique city to visit in Southeast Asia, Ho Chi Minh City is an attractive choice.

8 **Write an outline for an essay on one of the following topics or on a topic of your choice.**

a. health and medicine in your country

b. an important problem in your country

c. the importance of technology in society

9 **Edit your outline for unity and coherence, then write the essay.**

10 **Exchange the essay you wrote in exercise 9 above with a partner. Look for the use of the cohesive devices you have learned about in this unit.**

Review

11 These pairs of sentences need to be joined together to form English proverbs. Choose the best connecting word or phrase to connect each pair. Compare your answers with a partner, and then discuss the possible meaning of each proverb.

a. Don't count your chickens .... they hatch.

1. before **2.** so **3.** because

b. .... life gives you lemons, make lemonade.

1. Before **2.** When **3.** Because

c. Time flies .... you're having fun.

1. after **2.** although **3.** when

d. You can lead a horse to water, ... you can't make it drink.

1. and **2.** but **3.** or

e. Laugh, ... the world laughs with you. Cry, ... you cry alone.

1. and, but **2.** and, and **3.** but, but

f. You don't know what water is worth .... your well is dry.

1. because **2.** after **3.** until

g. .... the storm comes a calm.

1. after **2.** Because **3.** Since

h. Don't speak of my debts .... you intend to pay them.

1. however **2.** unless **3.** moreover

12 Think of one or two proverbs in your language and translate them into English. Share yours with the class. Then choose one of the proverbs and write a paragraph explaining its meaning.

12 *Essays For Examinations*

In this unit, you will learn ...

- **common instructions for essay tests.**
- **techniques for writing timed essays and managing time.**

➲ Essay tests

You may be asked to write essays for tests in your classes, or on entrance examinations for colleges and universities in English-speaking countries. You will have to write essays if you take the TOEFL (Test of English as a Foreign Language), the MELAB (Michigan English Language Assessment Battery), Cambridge Assessment (University of Cambridge International and ESOL Examinations), or the IELTS (International English Language Testing System). These essays are written at one sitting, in a limited amount of time.

Timed essays

1 **You probably already have some experience and ideas that will be useful to you when you write timed essays. Discuss the following questions with a partner or group.**

a. Have you ever written timed essays in your own language? Describe the situation(s).

b. Have you ever written timed essays in English? Describe the situation(s).

c. In what situations will you write timed essays in English in the future?

d. What are some ways that writing a timed essay is different from writing an essay without a time limit? Make a list. Then look at your list and say which aspects might be challenging for you.

e. Do you know any good techniques for writing timed essays? Share them with your partner or group.

Instructions for timed essays

➲ How to write good timed essays

- Check to see how many questions you must answer. Some exams may say *Choose three of the following five topics*. You will not receive a higher score if you write more than three essays—your instructor will probably just grade the first three.
- Check how many points the essay is worth. On a 100-point test, an essay worth twenty points should be longer and more detailed than one worth five points. Spend more time on the longer essays.
- Pay close attention to the instructions for each individual essay question. Be especially careful with questions that have several parts. It is helpful to underline or circle key instructions so that you do not leave anything out.

  Example:

  In your opinion, what is the Key difference between Chinese medicine and Western medicine? Illustrate this difference with one example.

- Use some of your time for planning (gathering and organizing ideas) and for proofreading your finished essay.
- Always write in complete sentences and pay careful attention to grammar and spelling. Don't experiment with structures or words you are not confident about using correctly.
- Write neatly. Instructors may give lower grades to essays they cannot read easily.

➲ Common instructions on essay tests

compare / contrast
As you learned in Unit 6, compare / contrast paragraphs talk about similarities and differences. You can write one paragraph to compare and another to contrast, or compare and contrast a different idea related to your topic in each paragraph.

discuss
This broad term invites you to describe different ideas about a topic. Organize your discussion around a central thesis statement.

explain, show how
These instructions ask you to show cause and effect. You may also find instructions like these for a problem / solution essay, as discussed in Unit 7.

show, describe, use examples
Make sure that you provide specific details to support your points, as you practiced in Unit 3.

which
This word asks you to make a choice. Often a question with *which* will also ask you to defend your choice, for example, *Which solution would you recommend, and why?* Make sure that you clearly indicate your choice in your answer. Don't try to write about each possibility.

2 **Underline the most important part of the instructions in these essay questions.**

Discuss your answers with a partner or group. Talk about what kinds of information you would include in your answer.

a. Compare and contrast public and private high school education in your country.

b. Think of a story you have read which has also been made into a movie. Describe the differences between the two versions.

c. Show how the rise in popularity of communication by cell phone has changed the ways in which young people communicate.

d. Discuss three results of the Norman conquest of Great Britain in 1066. Which do you feel was the most important?

e. Which environmental problem is the most significant in your community? Explain how your community can solve this problem.

Answering directly

➲ Essay test short cuts

Time is limited, so it is a good idea to take certain "short cuts" on essay tests. Most importantly, you should write a very short introduction—just one or two sentences is OK—which includes your thesis statement. Do not include the background information you might normally include in an essay. Make sure that your thesis statement directly answers the question. Your answer should show that you know the information that the test asks about. Extra information or any information that is not related to your topic will not help your grade. Your conclusion should also be brief.

3 **Underline the key words of this essay question.**

Which effect of the California gold rush do you think had the biggest impact on the character of San Francisco today?

4 **Check (✓) the introductions that answer the question in exercise 3 above directly. Write an ✗ by the ones that contain unnecessary information or do not directly address the question. Discuss your answers with a partner.**

a. ☐

San Francisco is a fascinating city with a very special character. Each year, thousands of tourists from the United States and other countries visit San Francisco to enjoy its unique style. Many important events contributed to the character of San Francisco, including the California gold rush, the earthquake of 1906, immigration from Mexico, and the rise of the computer industry. But the gold rush was the most important of these events.

b. ☐

The effect of the California gold rush that had the biggest impact on the character of San Francisco today was the damage done by the mining to the rivers and surrounding land.

➲ Write your topic sentences first

Some students like to first write the topic sentence for each main point on the answer sheet, leaving space to go back and fill in the details. If you choose this method, you can add information and examples to each paragraph until you finish or your time runs out. If you run out of time, you may leave out some details, but you won't leave out any main points.

Living alone is the best way for me to learn independence while I am in college.

One of the main benefits of living alone will be that I will learn to take care of myself by cooking my own food and doing my own housework and laundry.

Another benefit of living alone will be that I will learn to budget my money.

College is a time not only to study, but to learn to be an independent adult. Living alone will help me learn how to handle this responsibility.

6 **For one of the five-minute outlines you wrote for exercise 5 on page 92, write a topic sentence for each main point.**

Checking your work

➲ Check your work

After you finish your essay, or at least five minutes before your time is up, take some time to check your work. Read the essay from beginning to end. Although you cannot read your essay out loud (unless you are alone), try to "hear" what it would sound like in your head.

- Did you answer all parts of the question?
- Is your essay unified? Cross out any unrelated ideas.
- Are words spelled correctly and written neatly?
- Do your sentences sound clear? If you are not sure if your grammar is correct, try to say your ideas another way.
- Did you erase or cross out any mistakes or stray marks?

7 **You have already spent five minutes writing an outline for the topics in exercise 5 on page 92. Now choose one of those topics and spend another twenty minutes writing the essay. Then take five minutes to check your work. Then share your essay with a partner or small group.**

Review

8 Work in groups of four. Divide into pairs. Pair A, look at the essay on American and British English in Unit 8, exercise 1 on page 57. Pair B, look at the essay on Chinese medicine in Unit 11, exercise 1 on page 79. Do the following:

a. In pairs, write two or three essay questions about the information presented. Give your essay questions to the other pair.

b. Individually, choose one of the questions the other pair wrote for you and write an answer based on the information given in the essay. You may use your textbook. Write a thirty-minute essay in this way: First, write a five-minute outline. Then, write your essay for twenty minutes. Finally, spend five minutes checking your work.

c. Rejoin your group of four. Take turns reading your essays aloud. After one person reads the essay, the other group members should identify the thesis statement and main ideas. Tell the writer something you liked about the essay.

Additional Materials

Photocopiable Materials

Sample essay: brainstorming

Assignment: Write an argument essay of 2–3 pages. First, choose a topic and brainstorm some ideas. Then, organize your ideas into an outline. After you have checked your outline carefully, write the first draft of your essay. Exchange drafts with a classmate, and give and receive peer feedback. Using those comments to guide you, prepare a final draft.

Remember: all final papers must be typed and double-spaced! Please turn in your brainstorming, outline, and first draft together with your final draft.

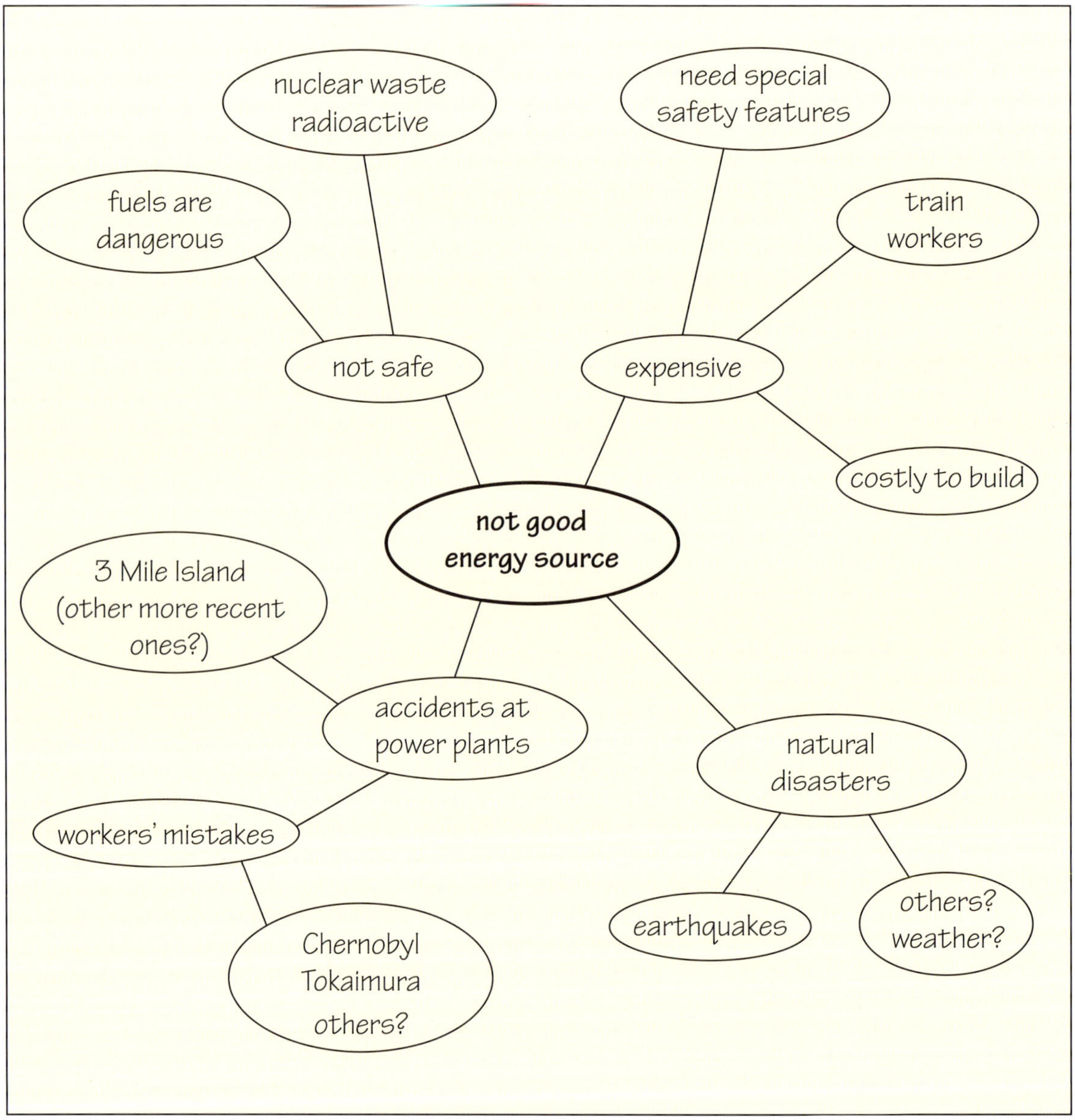

➲ **The outline for this sample essay appears on page 65.**

Sample essay: first draft

➲ **The comments on the essay were written by one of the writer's classmates.**

Don't Support Nuclear Energy!

Can you add some kind of introduction before giving your thesis statement?

Even though it can provide the world with a source of electricity, nuclear power is not a good energy source because it is too expensive, the materials used in the power plants are not safe, and there is a great possibility of accidents. *Good thesis statement—very clear*

Can you add a topic sentence to this paragraph?

First of all, nuclear fuel is expensive. It must be taken out of the ground and transported great distances. As fuels are used up, they will become even more expensive, just as oil and gas have become more expensive. In addition, nuclear power plants are expensive to build and to operate. It is expensive to train workers. *Can you explain this idea a little more?* *You have used "expensive" 5 times in the paragraph ...*

Needs transition

Nuclear materials are not safe. When uranium is taken out of the ground, radioactive gas is released. This is not safe for the miners. Uranium itself is also not safe. Being around uranium is not safe for workers. *Why is uranium not safe?*

Needs transition

Nuclear waste is also dangerous. It is very radioactive, and it is difficult to dispose of it or even to store it safely. *This is a very short paragraph ...*

Nice transition

Most significantly, there is always a possibility of nuclear accidents. The power plants themselves can fail when they get old or if they are not built correctly. The machinery can malfunction, too. In 1979, problems at the Three Mile Island nuclear power plant in the United States resulted in radioactive materials escaping into the nearby community. More recently, equipment failures were responsible for accidents in power plants in Darlington, Canada (1992) and Sellafield, England (2005). *Nice specific example* *Can you explain what happened at these places?*

Can you add a transition?

Workers at nuclear power plants can make mistakes. Perhaps the most famous of these incidents occurred at Chernobyl (in the former U.S.S.R.) in 1986. Radioactivity from the Chernobyl accident was recorded as far away as Eastern

Good detail

Europe, Scandinavia, and even Japan. Human error was responsible for power plant

Are these the only mistakes that have happened?

accidents in Tokaimura, Japan (1999) and Asco, Spain (2007–2008). There is no way we can guarantee that workers will not make mistakes again in the future.

Even natural disasters can affect nuclear power plants. A big storm in the

Can you give some comment about this?

Pacific Ocean in 1982 washed nuclear waste out into the ocean. Earthquakes are a threat, too. In 2011, a strong earthquake damaged several nuclear reactors in Fukushima, Japan.

It is true that oil and gas cannot supply all of the world's energy needs

Good restatement of thesis

much longer. However, we cannot replace them with an energy source that is too expensive and is dangerous from the time the fuels are taken out of the ground and even after the plant is running.

I think you need some kind of concluding sentence. What do you recommend instead of nuclear power?

Good essay! You have a lot of information and specific examples. Your arguments are very clear. Your organization is good, too.

Sample essay: second draft

Carol Chan
Academic Writing
Argument Essay, Second Draft
October 15, 2010

Don't Support Nuclear Energy!

These days, it seems like everyone is worried about how the world will meet its energy demands when we have run out of oil and natural gas. Scientists and researchers are investigating such power sources as solar energy, wind energy, and even energy from hot rocks beneath the earth's surface. However, there is one energy source that I believe should not be developed any further. In fact, I believe that we should stop using it as soon as possible. Even though it can provide the world with a source of electricity, nuclear power is not a good energy source because it is too expensive, the materials used in the power plants are not safe, and there is a great possibility of accidents.

Nuclear power is not an economical energy source. First of all, nuclear fuel is expensive. It must be taken out of the ground and transported great distances. As fuels are used up, they will become even more expensive, just as oil and gas have. In addition, nuclear power plants cost a lot of money to build and to operate because of the great care that must be taken with safety. Because the people who work in nuclear power plants must be highly trained specialists, salaries for workers are also high.

In addition to being expensive, nuclear materials are not safe. When uranium is taken out of the ground, radioactive gas is released. This is not safe for the miners. Uranium itself also is not safe because of its high radioactivity. Because of this, people who work with nuclear fuels are at risk of cancer. As nuclear power plants run, they create nuclear waste, which also is dangerous. It is very radioactive, and it is difficult to dispose of or even to store safely. No town wants nuclear waste buried nearby, and for good reason.

Most significantly, there is always a possibility of nuclear accidents. The power plants themselves can fail when they get old or if they are not built correctly. The machinery can malfunction, too. In 1979, problems at the Three Mile Island nuclear power plant in the United States resulted in radioactive materials escaping into the nearby community. More recently, equipment failures were responsible for accidents in power plants in Darlington, Canada, in 1992, and Sellafield, England, in 2005. Both of these accidents led to leaks of radioactive material.

It is not just buildings and equipment which can fail, but people, too. Workers at nuclear power plants can make mistakes. Perhaps the most famous of these incidents occurred at Chernobyl, in the former U.S.S.R., in 1986. Radioactivity from the Chernobyl accident was recorded as far away as Eastern Europe, Scandinavia, and even Japan. Human error has been responsible for numerous power plant accidents. Some recent well-known examples include Tokaimura, Japan, in 1999, where untrained, unqualified workers prepared some fuel incorrectly, and Asco, Spain, where a radioactive leak that started in 2007 was not reported until 2008. There is no way we can guarantee that workers will not make mistakes again in the future.

Even natural disasters can affect nuclear power plants. A big storm in the Pacific Ocean in 1981 washed nuclear waste from Mururoa out into the ocean. In 2011, a strong earthquake damaged several nuclear reactors in Fukushima, Japan. It is impossible for people to predict or to prevent events like this. Different types of severe weather or natural disasters can strike almost anywhere in the world and they can cause disastrous nuclear accidents.

It is true that oil and gas cannot supply all of the world's energy needs much longer. However, we must not replace them with another non-renewable energy source that is expensive and dangerous, from the time the fuels are taken out of the ground to even after the plant is running. Instead, we must develop cheaper and, most importantly, safer types of energy to power our world.

Punctuation

Here are some common rules for using punctuation in your writing. Of course, this is not a complete list. If you have further questions, check a grammar book or ask your teacher.

➲ Capitalization

Always capitalize:

- the first word of every sentence.
- days of the week (*Tuesday*) and months of the year (*April*).
- the first letter (only) of the names of people and places (*Bangkok*, *Ayaka Seo*).
- the main words of a title, but not articles (*a*, *an*, *the*) or prepositions (words like *to*, *of*, *for*) or conjunctions (*and*, *but*), unless they are the first word in the title:
  The Three Things I Do in the Morning

➲ Period (.)

A period comes at the end of a statement:

An electronic dictionary is more convenient than a paper one.

If the sentence ends with an abbreviation, don't use more than one period:

RIGHT: My mother just finished her Ph.D.

WRONG: My mother just finished her Ph.D..

➲ Comma (,)

Use a comma to separate a series of three or more items:

I take a dictionary, a notebook, and some paper to class every day.

Use a comma before words like *and, but, or, so,* and *yet* to separate two parts of a sentence that each have a subject and a verb.

She needed some work experience, *so* she got a part-time job.

He did not study at all, *but* he still got an 87 on the test.

Use a comma after an introductory word or expression, such as *However, Therefore,* and *In conclusion*:

However, the high price of electric cars means that most people cannot afford one.

➲ Quotation marks (" ")

Use quotation marks when you handwrite the title of a book or movie:

"Hamlet" was written by Shakespeare.

When you use a word processor, you should use italics instead:

Hamlet was written by Shakespeare.

Use quotation marks to show the exact words someone spoke or wrote:

The professor announced, "We're going to have an exam next week."

Shakespeare wrote, "All the world's a stage."

Do not use quotation marks if you're reporting what another person said:

The professor said that we should study hard this week.

Note: *That*, as used in the sentence above, usually indicates that the remark is not a direct quotation.

➲ Punctuation when using quotation marks

If you are using expressions like *he said* or *the girl remarked* after the quotation, then use a comma and not a period at the end of the quoted sentence:

"We're going to have an exam next week," announced the professor.

Use a period if the quoted sentence comes at the end:

The professor announced, "We're going to have an exam next week."

Notice how a comma is used after *announced*, above, to introduce the quotation.

Periods and commas are placed inside quotation marks. Exclamation points and question marks may come inside or outside, depending on whether they are part of the quotation or part of the surrounding sentence:

"Do you know who wrote *Hamlet*?" asked the teacher.

Do you know who said "All the world's a stage"?

➲ Quotation marks and capitalization

Capitalize the first letter of the word that begins a quotation. However, if an expression like *she said* interrupts the quotation and divides the sentence, then do not capitalize the first word of the part that finishes the quotation:

"Next week," said the professor, "we are going to have an exam."

The comma after *week* separates the quotation from the test of the sentence.

Use a capital letter only if the second part is a new, complete sentence:

"We'll have an exam next week," explained the teacher. "It will take thirty minutes."

➲ Advice for academic writing

The following are not usually used in academic writing, although they are fine in informal situations, such as letters to your friends.

- Parentheses that give information which is not part of your main sentence:

  Cell phones are useful (and besides, I think they look great).

  If your idea is important, it should be in a sentence of its own. If it is not important, it should not be in your paper.

- The abbreviation *etc.* to continue a list. Instead, use a phrase like *such as* in your sentence:

  Students in my university come from countries such as China, India, and Australia.

- Exclamation points (!). Instead, write strong sentences with plenty of details to show your reader your feelings:

  Angel Falls is one of the most spectacular natural wonders you will ever see.

- An ellipsis (…) at the end of a sentence, to show that the sentence is not finished:

  The professor said that I should study hard, so …

  Instead, finish your sentence:

  The professor said that I should study, so I should not go to the party tonight.

Sample information letter

10-6-14-105 Sakura-cho ← *Sender's address*
Setagaya-ku
Tokyo, Japan 332-3322
E-mail: sakura@ttt.ne.jp

February 15, 2011 ← *Date the letter was written*

Admissions Office ← *Receiver's address*
Central Michigan University
Mt. Pleasant, MI 48859
U.S.A.

To Whom It May Concern: ← *Greeting*

I am writing to express an interest in the Intensive English Program at your university, which I learned of while searching on the Internet. ← *Introduction*

I would appreciate any information you could provide about your program. I am interested in studying English for one semester, so I would like to know more about the courses your offer, the number of hours of study per week, and the tuition cost.

In addition, it would be helpful if you could provide information about housing. I am interested in learning as much as I can about the culture, so if it is possible, I would like to live with a family.

(Body)

Thank you in advance for your time and help. I look forward to receiving more information about your program. ← *Conclusion*

Sincerely, ← *Closing*

Shinichi Usuda ← *Signature*

Shinichi Usuda ← *Sender's name*

Sample statement of purpose

➲ What is a statement of purpose?

When you apply to a college or university in the United States for an undergraduate or graduate degree, you are often asked to write a one-page statement of purpose. This is a short essay that tells the university why you are applying, and also why you would be a good addition to their program. The essay below is from a Taiwanese student wishing to enter a Master's Degree (M.A.) program in Teaching English as a Second Language at Western Arizona University in the United States.

I have been interested in English since I was twelve, when my family took a trip to Australia. I thought then how useful and exciting it would be to talk to the people I met. It was not only the Australians who spoke English, but also other tourists we met who had traveled there from all over the world. Whether they were from Germany, Indonesia, or Brazil, their common language was English, and I wanted to share that language with them.

I worked hard at my English studies in junior high school and high school. I was a member of our school's English Conversation Club, and in my last year I was secretary of the club. I also took part in the national English Speech Contest for three years.

In college, I majored in English literature. I also took English conversation lessons at a private school two evenings a week. In addition, I made friends with some of the international students at my college, and we always spoke together in English. During my last two years at college, I took a part-time job tutoring elementary and junior high school students in English grammar and conversation.

Because of my long interest in English and my experience teaching English, I am sure that I would like to become an ESL teacher. I have chosen to study in the United States so that I can also learn about the culture of an English-speaking country. I have heard about Western Arizona University from other graduates, and I am impressed with the classes offered there and the quality of instruction. I think I would be a valuable addition to your ESL program because I could share my own experiences with learning English. I look forward to the opportunity to further my own knowledge of English and of American culture, and to meeting the challenges of both learning and teaching with the other students in your program.

Sample résumé

TITIRAT JINAPHAN
225 Soi Pracharak 33
Phachachuen Road
Don Muang
Bangkok, Thailand 10210
Tel. (662) 954-8081
E-mail: tj26@bangkok.com

WORK OBJECTIVE

To obtain a job working in management and marketing for an international company.

EDUCATION

CENTRAL MICHIGAN UNIVERSITY, Mt. Pleasant, Michigan, U.S.A., May 2011
Master of Science in Administration
Concentration: General Administration (Business Management and Marketing)
Activities: World Connection Program (matches international students and American students for language and cultural exchanges), Family Friendship Program (introduction to American lifestyle and culture)

THAMMASAT UNIVERSITY, Bangkok, Thailand, February 2008
Bachelor of Law (J.D. equivalent)
Activities: Law Students' Organization, Soccer Team

OTHER CERTIFICATES

CENTRAL MICHIGAN UNIVERSITY, Mt. Pleasant, Michigan, U.S.A., December 2010
SAP R/3 Enterprise Software Certificate (integrated enterprise software applications)

ENGLISH LANGUAGE INSTITUTE, Mt. Pleasant, Michigan, U.S.A., May 2009
Certificate from the English Language Program for International Students at Central Michigan University

WORK EXPERIENCE

CENTRAL MICHIGAN UNIVERSITY, Mt. Pleasant, Michigan, U.S.A., September 2010–May 2011

Computer Lab Assistant
- Assisted in maintaining lab equipment.
- Responsible for answering questions for the Computer Help Desk.
- Provided assistance to students using the lab.

SAPAKORN, Nakhonsawan, Thailand (Corporate Farming Business), April 2004–May 2008

Personal Assistant to the Owners / Sales Representative
- Responsible for sales and delivery of farming materials and supplies to farmers.
- Conducted banking and financial transactions, including payroll distribution.
- Coordinated and supervised staff of ten in janitorial and materials management.
- Developed and analyzed marketing strategies for the sales of agricultural products.
- Arranged and executed the purchase of inventory essential to business.

ADDITIONAL SKILLS

Languages: Thai (native), English (fluent, both written and oral).
Computer: Lexis-Nexis, Westlaw, Microsoft Office, SPSS, SAP Enterprise Software, Internet Applications.

Peer feedback – paragraph

Writer's name: ....

Reader's name: ....

Assignment: ....

1. What is the topic of the paragraph? What is the main idea?

2. Does the paragraph have a topic sentence? If so, write it here:

3. Does each sentence support the topic sentence? If not, which sentence or sentences do not belong?

4. Does the paragraph have a concluding sentence? If so, does it restate the topic sentence or sum up the information?

5. Are there any places where the writer could add more details? Do you have any questions for the writer?

6. What are some good things about this paragraph?

PHOTOCOPIABLE

© Macmillan Publishers Limited, 2011. This page may be photocopied and used within the class.

Peer feedback – essay

Writer's name: ....

Reader's name: ....

Assignment: ....

1. What is the topic of the essay? What is the main idea?

2. Read the introduction. Is it interesting? Does it give some background information? Does it include a thesis statement? If so, write it here:

3. Does each body paragraph support the thesis statement? Write the topic sentence of each body paragraph here:

4. Are there any places where the writer could add more details? Do you have any questions for the writer?

5. Is there a conclusion to the essay? Does it restate the thesis or sum up the information or flow logically from the ideas in the essay? Does it contain any new points?

6. What are some good things about this essay?

© Macmillan Publishers Limited, 2011. This page may be photocopied and used within the class.

PHOTOCOPIABLE

Macmillan Education
4 Crinan Street
London N1 9XW
A division of Macmillan Publishers Limited
Companies and representatives throughout the world

ISBN 978-0-2304-1592-8

Text © Dorothy E Zemach and Lisa A Ghulldu 2011
Design and illustration © Macmillan Publishers Limited 2011

First published 2003

All rights reserved; no part of this publication may be reproduced, stored in a retrieval system, transmitted in any form, or by any means, electronic, mechanical, photocopying, recording, or otherwise, without the prior written permission of the publishers.

Note to Teachers

Photocopies may be made, for classroom use, of pages 106 and 107 without the prior written permission of Macmillan Publishers Limited. However, please note that the copyright law, which does not normally permit multiple copying of published material, applies to the rest of this book.

Designed by xen
Illustrated by Jackson Graham, Sophie Grillet, Stuart Perry, Val Saunders
Cover design by xen based on a design by Jackie Hill at 320 Design
Cover illustration/photograph by xen

Authors' acknowledgements

Dorothy E Zemach thanks students in the Academic English for International Students writing courses at the University of Oregon, who tried out many of the exercises in the book and provided valuable comments and suggestions.

Lisa A Ghulldu thanks Lisa von Reichbauer, instructor in the English Language Institute at Central Michigan University and the students in the Intensive English program who kindly helped pilot many of the exercises in the book and provided helpful comments and suggestions.

The publishers would like to thank the following for their assistance in the development of this course (in alphabetical order):

Chris Cottam, David Parker, Gordon Robson, Maria-Luiza Santos

The authors and publishers would like to thank the following for permission to reproduce their photographs:

Alamy p7(t),66,75(l), 76, 84Alamy / Travel Ink p11;
Bananastock p30;
Corbis pp75(t), 78/79, 86;
Getty pp15, 26/27, 28(bl), 33, 37, 57, 65, 68/67, 75(bc);
Photodisc pp17, 25(r), 38, 43(b), 58, 92;
Superstock pp25(l), 25(br), 32, 41, 60, 43(t),75(r), Superstock / Glow p14.

These materials may contain links for third party websites. We have no control over, and are not responsible for, the contents of such third party websites. Please use care when accessing them.

Although we have tried to trace and contact copyright holders before publication, in some cases this has not been possible. If contacted we will be pleased to rectify any errors or omissions at the earliest opportunity.

Printed and bound in Thailand

2018 2017 2016 2015
13 12 11 10 9 8 7